HK Phil 50+

HK Phil 50+

Jimmy Shiu

港樂 HKPhil

HKU PRESS 香港大學出版社

Made possible through the sponsorship of HK Phil Principal Clarinet Andrew Simon (1988–present) in memory of his mother, Mrs Regina Simon.

Contents

Foreword

Before it became a professional orchestra in 1974, the Hong Kong Philharmonic Orchestra was an amateur society, founded to bring together classical music enthusiasts of different social groups in Hong Kong. This book tells the remarkable story of how, in just half a century, it became a leading international orchestra.

The orchestra's development has, in many ways, mirrored the rise of its home, Hong Kong: it drew on the best of both Western and Chinese talent, yet developed its own unique culture. The story of the orchestra is really the story of the people who supported it – the players, the conductors, the management, the sponsors and of course the audience. We are deeply indebted to Jimmy Shiu, our former audience development manager, for telling the story of those people in this book. In the following pages, he traces the orchestra's rise over the past fifty years (and more), sharing a wealth of anecdotes garnered from behind the scenes.

In any story there are important turning points. One very significant one for the HK Phil was its four-year journey through recording Wagner's *Ring* cycle under our previous music director, Maestro Jaap van Zweden, which won praise from critics around the world and in 2019 made us the first orchestra in Asia to be awarded 'Orchestra of the Year' by the prestigious UK classical music magazine *Gramophone*. A more recent turning point came in our 50th season, we announced the appointment of the brilliant Finnish conductor Tarmo Peltokoski as our next music director: our eagerly-awaited first recording with him will be released in the 2025/26 season.

That the orchestra came this far was due as much to the ensemble off the stage as on the stage. We have been fortunate to have a number of long-term friends on this journey: the HK Phil would not exist today without the kind support we receive from our generous sponsors and donors. Though I cannot list them all, I would like to thank two in particular. We have been the fortunate beneficiaries of the HKSAR Government's vision and commitment: it realised many years ago that an international city needed international cultural institutions and was willing to invest to develop them. Through the Culture, Sports and Tourism Bureau, the Leisure and Cultural Services Department and their predecessors, it was the earliest and most committed of the HK Phil's supporters: one could not ask for a better partner. We are also deeply grateful to our principal patron, the Swire Group, that has since 2006 supported the HK Phil's vision and mission.

I would like to say a special word of thanks to Andy Simon, our principal clarinet, who generously sponsored the production of the English edition of this book. Few people have a longer history with, or a deeper commitment to the HK Phil: he has brought almost four decades of passion and energy to the orchestra.

An orchestra exists, above all, for its audience: the friends for whom it plays each week. While commemorating our fiftieth anniversary, I would like to thank all the audiences that have supported and encouraged the orchestra over the decades. I hope this 50th anniversary publication will bring you pleasant memories of everything the HK Phil has achieved so far, and I hope it inspires us to achieve yet more in the years to come.

David Cogman
Chairman, Board of Governors
The Hong Kong Philharmonic Society Limited

Preface

The date was 31 January 1978.[1] Some fifteen members of my school's music club were invited to attend a concert at St. Paul's Convent School. In those days, it was uncommon for boys' school students to visit a girls' school. With some excitement, we stepped into the grand school hall. As we moved towards the first row (graciously reserved for us), it was nerve-racking to be gazed upon by hundreds of girls seated quietly, waiting for the concert to start.

I had only heard of the Hong Kong Philharmonic Orchestra (HK Phil) before, but now, their fifty to sixty musicians were right in front of me. Just one step forward, and I could have shaken hands with the concertmaster. That was amazing! But the more overwhelming moment was yet to come . . .

A charming lady appeared on stage and eloquently introduced the programme in English. I heard my schoolmates murmuring enthusiastically, 'Wow! Miss Hong Kong!' Then I realised that standing right before my very eyes was Ethel Lau, the second runner-up of the Miss Hong Kong Pageant of 1973.

I must say, aside from the feelings of being a boy in a girls' school and bumping into Miss Hong Kong – I have little recollection of what happened at the concert. There were about five pieces, one of which was narrated by Ethel. That could have been Benjamin Britten's *The Young Person's Guide to the Orchestra*. The programme sheet was in English. The only tune I knew was *Dance of the Yao People*. That was courtesy of my second-oldest brother, a school band clarinettist who kept playing the tune at home! I cannot recall who the conductor was. I have found no information in the orchestra's archive. However, in that particular season, the Principal Conductor and Music Director

[1] The exact date of that concert was provided by my elder brother, who has been keeping a diary since school days. He was then-chairman of the music club and leader of that visit.

Hans Günter Mommer frequently brought the orchestra to schools. I may have had the good fortune of watching him live!

Looking back, that first encounter with the orchestra was in fact a prelude to my magical HK Phil journey.

Four years later, I was a fervent music-lover and attended HK Phil's concerts regularly. I preferred to sit in the first row (partly for a 'nostalgic' St. Paul's Convent feel, and partly because the ticket price was the lowest). Once, Benedict Cruft, the first associate concertmaster, nodded to this 'loyal fan', which made me feel that I was part of the orchestra.

Ten years later, that was not just a feeling. After finishing my master's studies, I successfully applied to be the orchestra's audience development manager. The guy who enthusiastically clapped for the musicians was now their colleague! And forty-plus years later, I am writing a book to commemorate the HK Phil's 50th anniversary, which came with a chance to interview that Miss Hong Kong contestant – Ethel!

Like me, thousands of music lovers have their own HK Phil stories. This book is a compilation of these stories, which I hope may further enlighten us about our orchestra, orchestral music in general, and the development of music in Hong Kong.

Fifty Dishes

To publish this book, I gathered stories from interviews, old documents, clippings, and printed materials, among other media. I grouped similar content such as ticket prices, performance venues, the orchestra's recordings, soloists, audience development, and pop concerts into separate categories. Then, twenty-two main dishes were cooked up from the ingredients, accompanied by twenty-eight bite-size titbits, making it fifty!

50+

This book marks the 50th anniversary of HK Phil as a professional performance body. However, it also touches on its predecessors.

The Sino-British Orchestra (SBO) was inaugurated in 1947 and gave its first concert the following year. In 1957, HK Phil was founded and most former SBO members became HK Phil players. The orchestra operated for seventeen years before turning professional in 1974. To find out more about the relationship between SBO and HK Phil, please read 港樂血緣報告 ('Hong Kong Philharmonic Orchestra's Bloodline', an online article in Chinese) written by Mr Leon Chu.

Since HK Phil's roots go back to 1947 (even 1946 – the year when its parent organisation Sino-British Society was established), I was tempted to make it a '50+' book to include titbits from those twenty-seven pre-professional years.

Almost eighty years is a long period to cover within the span of this book. I have chosen breadth over depth: the presentation is eclectic and rather achronological and much of its content is concise, while staying focused on the subjects of the respective chapters, leaving room for remarks and observations. Having said that, the spectrum is still too wide. There are many more people whom I did not have a chance to talk to and a wealth of further information I would have liked to include.

Coda

It's an honour to be the writer of this book. At the same time, I am grateful that this has indubitably been a group project. I have assumed the role of an arranger, compiling tunes by music connoisseurs into an orchestral suite for your appreciation. Enjoy!

Jimmy Shiu
1 March 2025

1 *Evolution of the Outfit*

The Hong Kong Philharmonic Orchestra – HK Phil – is not a disciplinary force and does not mandate a uniform. However, players (especially men) often adhere to a similar set of attire when appearing on stage. What players wear has evolved, reflecting changes in aesthetics, in the availability of resources, in the nature of the concerts, and in social customs. Look at Photo 1.1. Gentlemen are mostly in white shirts and long white trousers, and the lady is in a long black dress (if white is white and black is black – my assumption on looking at a black-and-white photograph).

Photo 1.1: One of SBO's earliest pictures, taken at the orchestra's first concert in 1948. The conductor was Solomon Bard.

Photo 1.2: SBO conducted by Alastair Blair-Kerr along with solo pianist Caroline Braga performing at St. Stephen's Girls' College in 1952.

In a Western orchestra, there are usually more variations in what ladies wear. The current dress code for HK Phil's female players is 'all-black, long dress or trousers, and tops with sleeves'. What male players wear is more undeviating. During the Sino-British era, however, it could be quite flexible. Take Photo 1.2 (from 1952) as an example. Everyone was dressed up for the occasion. There were, however, black bow ties, long ties, black socks, white socks, blazers in black, white, and other colours, no blazers . . . all appearing at the same time.

The Humphrey Bogart Look

In the following years, female players continued to sport long black dresses. At times, it was a combination of black and white; there was also a picture with a lady in *cheongsam*, which reflected the 'Sino' in the Sino-British Orchestra (the SBO – which later became HK Phil). As for gentlemen, sometimes it was a black suit. White blazers and black trousers were once customary, too. Incidentally, this was the dress code of the New York Philharmonic's visit to Hong Kong in July 2023, with ladies in white tops and black trousers. This classic look reminds me of Humphrey Bogart in the movie *Casablanca*, and this is a common outfit for jazz bands. Resident Conductor Lio Kuokman told me that it was the standard appearance of an American orchestra when performing outdoors. Unsurprising, as that's exactly what he wore at the 2023 Swire Symphony Under the Stars, where he directed the orchestra and played in George Gershwin's *Rhapsody in Blue*.

Photo 1.3: Lio Kuokman at the 2023 Swire Symphony Under the Stars concert.

Photo 1.4: HK Phil and its first Music Director Lim Kek-tjiang.

White Tie

As the white blazer fell out of use, black suits (or tuxedos) with black bow-ties became the standard for male players. In Photo 1.4, taken around the time the orchestra turned professional in 1974, one can see Music Director and Principal Conductor Lim Kek-tjiang in a long tailcoat (usually with a white bow tie: the 'white tie' outfit), while other players remained in 'black tie'.

In 1983, the orchestra had the honour of being invited to play at the Osaka International Music Festival. HK Phil's name was listed along with distinguished groups such as the National Symphony Orchestra from Washington DC, the Vienna Philharmonic Orchestra, the NHK Symphony Orchestra from Japan, and the Royal Ballet from the UK.

Photo 1.5: HK Phil appearing at the Osaka International Music Festival, 1983.

Even so, apart from conductor Kenneth Schermerhorn, all gentlemen from the Hong Kong 'legion' were in black suits and black ties.

The Turning Point

In 1988, the orchestra's Ladies' Committee set up a fundraising event – the Vienna Opera Ball. The venue was lavishly decorated to welcome distinguished celebrity guests. For this glamorous occasion, the Ladies' Committee generously arranged for a tailcoat with a white bow tie to be tailor-made for every performing gentleman. Apparently, each set cost HK$4,000. Since then, the white tie has remained a fixture to this day.

Photo 1.6: Music Director Kenneth Schermerhorn leading the orchestra at the Vienna Opera Ball as players make their white tie debut in 1988.

Photo 1.7: The ceremony announcing Swire Group as principal patron of the HK Phil, 12 April 2006, with Artistic Director and Chief Conductor Edo de Waart and HK Phil members. It was too hot inside the marquee. Male players were allowed to take off their tailcoats.

Down Dress

There were 'down dress' times too. At a concert in Bangkok in 1983, there was suddenly no air-conditioning in the hall. Conductor Kenneth Schermerhorn instructed musicians to take off their blazers for the performance. A similar incident happened at HK Phil's season finale on 8 July 2006. The device that pumped sea-water into the air-conditioning system failed. Conductor Gianluigi Gelmetti called on players not to put on their blazers, and the band gave a 'blazing' performance.

At the 2024 Swire Symphony Under the Stars, it was for another reason that the blazers were not put on. On the first night, 16 November 2024, the show was met with torrential rain. Players and conductor Elim Chan performed in raincoats!

Half-naked Performance

Players usually wear shirts and ties for concerts in schools. But according to Ambrose Law, a percussionist in the 1970s, the toughest test was to perform at schools during high summer. Back then, most school halls were not air-conditioned and it was akin to playing inside a furnace. Orchestra members raised in south China may have been able to bear it; however, for expatriates coming from cooler climates, the heat was torture. Once the concertmaster even took off his shirt and played half-naked!

Jeans and T-shirts

Formal wear is not the most comfortable attire. Players do dress casually when it comes to a family concert. As the title 'Swire Denim Series' suggests, everyone puts on their jeans, walking shoes and T-shirts

Photo 1.8: The 2013 Swire Denim Series: Baroque @ 9 O'clock concert featured Conductor Julian Wachner and Cellist Jian Wang. Orchestra members wore colourful T-shirts, creating a lively, relaxed atmosphere that set the tone as soon as audiences entered the concert hall.

Photo 1.9: The 2017 Swire Denim Series: Final Fantasy: Final Symphony concert blended the iconic video game series with classical music. After the performance, Conductor Philip Chu and Pianist Mischa Cheung took photos with audience members dressed as characters from the game.

Photo 1.10: HK Phil's first overseas tour in 1980. On the far right is Julia Hsiao (acting concertmaster). Her balloon style trousers are certainly eye-catching.

provided by Chevignon. This easier look goes well with easier listening music.

In Costume

The first overseas tour that HK Phil undertook was in September 1980, when they accompanied the Sadler's Wells Royal Ballet (now the Royal Birmingham Ballet) to Malaysia and Thailand. For the single-act ballet *Elite Syncopations* – set to Scott Joplin's music, arranged by Sir Kenneth MacMillan – players were on stage instead of in the pit. They wore striped shirts, braces, and round-brimmed hats – special costumes which brought the audience back to the ragtime era in the United States at the turn of the twentieth century.

Of all the costumes the orchestra have put on, I found it most memorable when Magic Circle Mime Co. were the featured artists. It was Halloween. The stage was darkened in the first half, setting a spooky scene. When the second half began, an unsettling figure came onto the stage. With ragged hair, a bandaged body, and crutches, he stared and giggled at the audience. Look closer! Yes, it was First Associate Concertmaster Leung Kin-fung. Other players joined, making their way through the audience onto the stage. There were Mercurochrome-steeped bandages, vampire teeth, pirate hats, and exaggerated makeup. Principal Timpani James Boznos even wore broken drum-frame around his body. The house filled with cheers and thunderous applause. Conversely, that special attire also left a chilling impression on my little boy, who to this day is still not a fan of Halloween!

An outfit is an expression. To me, those two times were the most expressive!

2 *Making the 'Rite' Move . . .*

To an orchestra, whether it is their first or *n*th time playing Igor Stravinsky's *Le sacre du printemps* ('The Rite of Spring'), it will always feel like going in for an exam. When did HK Phil first become a 'candidate'?

How Revolutionary Is It?

The ballet *The Rite of Spring* opened a new sonic world to audiences, players, composers, conductors, and even Hollywood's music producers. This revolutionary work literally caused a riot among audience members during its world premiere at the Théâtre des Champs-Elysées in 1913. The composer sneaked away through a backstage window, and the Paris police had to help restore order on site.

Photo 2.1: Poster of the 2013 performance of *The Rite of Spring.*

With more than a century having passed, the work can no longer be considered avant-garde. After all, as early as 1940, Disney featured it in the animated movie *Fantasia* – an all-time family favourite. Excerpts of it can be heard occasionally in black-and-white Hong Kong movies of the 1950s and 1960s.

Having said that, its popularity has not made the piece easier to play. To conductors and players, each performance is a new challenge.

On 31 May and 1 June 2013, HK Phil joined the world in marking the one-hundredth anniversary of the work's premiere. Conductor Oleg Caetani's way of meeting the challenge was to do it from memory. That was impressive. By the way, his father, the celebrated Maestro Igor Markevitch, also had no music score in front of him when he conducted the same piece.

Before and since that centenary celebration, the orchestra have played it a few times. The most recent performance was on 20 and 21 September 2024. Conductor Vasily Petrenko added extra flavour to the work by programming Frederick Delius's *On Hearing the First Cuckoo in Spring* before the piece. Without a break, Stravinsky's piece came in and the audience had a surprising taste of how an English spring season was seamlessly transported into an ancient Russian one. (According to the composer's original concept, this was to be an ancient springtime when pagan sacrifice was practised.)

On 9 and 11 November 2006, the work was featured in a HK Phil concert as part of the New Vision Arts Festival presented by the Leisure and Cultural Services Department. On 1 March 2008, the orchestra collaborated with The Hong Kong Academy for Performing Arts, providing an opportunity for students and professional players to sit side by side. On 31 May and 2 June 2019, HK Phil players found themselves in the pit of the Hong Kong Cultural Centre Grand Theatre, and dancers from the Hong Kong Ballet were on stage to bring back the original form of the work – a ballet rather than a concert piece.

So, back to that question, when did HK Phil first play *The Rite of Spring*?

The answer is: 28 January 1983.

The Rite of Spring was seventy years old then; but the professional age of the orchestra was under ten. Most players had not played the piece before. Principal Second Violin Fan Ting did have the 'rite' experience, having left the orchestra temporarily to study at the Curtis Institute of Music in the United States from 1977 to 1980.

What are the challenges posed by *The Rite of Spring*? First, the rhythm. As HK Phil's current Second Associate Concertmaster Wang Liang explains, 'With the rapid changes of time signatures, one cannot simply count during the performance. The right "muscle memory" has to be cultivated through lengthy practice.'

The piece also has extreme ranges of pitch for many instruments: for example, in the very first bar the principal bassoon has to play that soft high C with special care. Everyone else has a rest bar. Playing an 'exposed' passage such as this one can be a daunting experience.

Other challenges include unexpected accents and enormous loudness. For the 1983 HK Phil premiere, there was also the practical need to look for many extra players and fit the augmented ensemble onto the stage at Hong Kong City Hall, which was not yet extended at that time.

Quick Fix

Instrument availability also posed an issue. The full score calls for two Wagner tubas and a bass trumpet, which HK Phil did not have. As its name suggests, the Wagner tuba was an instrument created for the performance of the composer's *Ring* cycle. It only rarely appears in works by other composers. At that time, even if the orchestra had been able to quickly order two Wagner tubas, it was not easy to find suitable players. The Wagner tuba parts were replaced by two horns; the bass trumpet was replaced by a trombone.

That 1983 'exam' went well. The audience showed great appreciation for the mastery of conductor Varujan Kojian and the hard work of the orchestra members. In a review published in the *New Evening Post*, Yu Siu-wah noted that although there were flaws, as the piece progressed, players became increasingly engrossed in their music-making and delivered a moving performance.

That was an impressive Hong Kong premiere. An excerpt of the piece was soon featured in HK Phil's school concert programme. Thus the work was canonised in HK Phil's repertoire.

This epic piece has been played at least in six more programmes, falling in the months of March, May, June, September, November, and January. On top of *The Rite of Spring*, we might have had 'The Rite of Summer', 'The Rite of Autumn', and 'The Rite of Winter'!

Opus Magnus

Some works are too massive to be staged in most venues, meaning that they are rarely heard live. The orchestra took part in arguably the most colossal one.

In celebration of the City Hall's twentieth birthday in 1982, Sir David Willcocks and the English Bach Choir came to Hong Kong and presented a few monumental choral works, including the Hong Kong premiere of the Berlioz Requiem. The orchestra became part of a gigantic performance force in taking on the biggest challenge in its history. There were twenty-three freelance musicians. The larger-than-normal ensemble was further augmented by young musicians from the Hong Kong Youth Symphony Orchestra, sharing desks with HK Phil's players. There were more wind players from Buddhist Tai Kwong Middle School, the 1st and 2nd Gurkha Rifles Regimental Band, the Hong Kong Lutheran Youth Band, the Hong Kong Youth Symphonic Band, Po Leung Kuk C. F. A. No. 1 College, the Royal Hong Kong Regiment (Volunteers) Band, and musicians from St. Bonaventure College and High School. Many local choirs joined voices with the English Bach Choir. The sonic effect at Queen Elizabeth Stadium must have been incredible.

Sir David also brought us Benjamin Britten's *War Requiem*, which was new to most music-lovers in Hong Kong. During World War II, Coventry Cathedral was badly damaged in the Blitz. Britten composed the choral masterpiece for the consecration of the new cathedral in 1962. Twenty years later, HK Phil gave its Hong Kong premiere. The scale was big but not to the extent of the Berlioz Requiem, making it possible for the performance to take place at the better-sounding City Hall Concert Hall. Members of the Hong Kong Children's Choir sang from one of the VIP boxes. The effect was ethereal!

HK Phil's second performance of the *War Requiem* is worth mentioning too.

On 7 November 2013, to mark the centenary year of Britten's birth of Britten (born 22 November 1913), a performance of the piece was given at the Cultural Centre Concert Hall. The sound of a pipe organ was heard, and the Hong Kong Children's Choir provided another delightful sound effect: doors of one of the audience entrances were let open to allow their celestial voices to enter the hall.[1] This time the conductor was Lorin Maazel; it was sadly the maestro's last collaboration with HK Phil before his death in 2014.

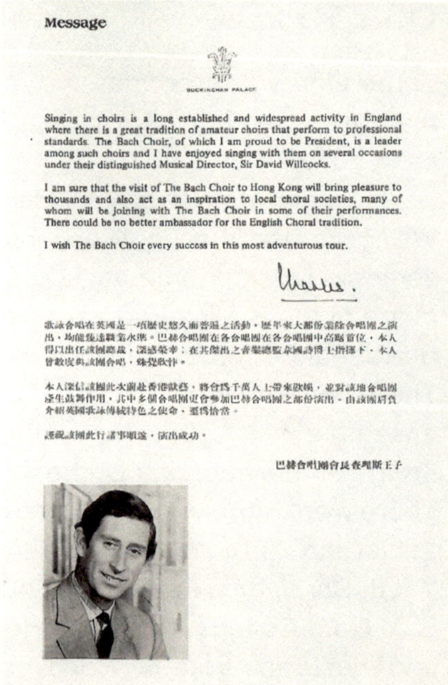

Message

BUCKINGHAM PALACE

Singing in choirs is a long established and widespread activity in England where there is a great tradition of amateur choirs that perform to professional standards. The Bach Choir, of which I am proud to be President, is a leader among such choirs and I have enjoyed singing with them on several occasions under their distinguished Musical Director, Sir David Willcocks.

I am sure that the visit of The Bach Choir to Hong Kong will bring pleasure to thousands and also act as an inspiration to local choral societies, many of whom will be joining with The Bach Choir in some of their performances. There could be no better ambassador for the English Choral tradition.

I wish The Bach Choir every success in this most adventurous tour.

Charles.

歌詠合唱在英國是一項歷史悠久而普遍之活動，歷年來大部份業餘合唱團之演出，均能達到職業水準。巴赫合唱團在各合唱團在各合唱團中高踞首位，本人得以出任該團總裁，深感榮幸；在其傑出之音樂總監韋爾確斯爵士指揮下，本人曾數度與該團合唱，殊覺欣忭。

本人深信該團此次前赴香港獻藝，將會為千萬人士帶來歡娛，並對該地合唱團產生鼓舞作用，其中多個合唱團更會參加巴赫合唱團之部份演出。由該團肩負介紹英國歌詠傳統特色之使命，至為恰當。

謹祝該團此行諸事順遂，演出成功。

巴赫合唱團會長查理斯王子

Photo 2.2: A message from the then-Prince Charles appeared in the Berlioz Requiem programme of 1982.

Turangalîla

While large-scale performances pose certain kinds of logistical problems, HK Phil has faced

[1] City Hall Concert Hall does not have a pipe organ; when the instrument is called for, the concert presenter usually rents an electric one.

others. In the case of one particular work, the first hurdle to overcome was finding the right pianist; the second hurdle was getting hold of a rare instrument, the ondes martenot.

In Olivier Messiaen's *Turangalîla-Symphonie*, the piano solo part is played quite differently (for example with extensive exploration of the instrument's top register) from that of a typical concerto. Not too many pianists are familiar with the part. And before an orchestra ever considers presenting the work, the first thing is to make sure the ondes martenot, and a qualified player, are available. The piece's Hong Kong premiere was given by the City of Birmingham Symphony Orchestra in 1991. HK Phil's rendition happened thirty-two years later in 2023. At that performance, the conductor was Jaap van Zweden. The pianist was Jean-Yves Thibaudet, and the ondes martenot was played by Cynthia Millar.

Photo 2.3: The 2023 Turangalîla-Symphonie concert.

Photo 2.4: Cynthia Millar introducing her ondes martenot to the concert audience.

After the concert, Millar stayed on stage to introduce her ondes martenot to the crowd. Her instrument is unique, to say the least – she tours the world with her loyal 'stage partner' every year, almost exclusively playing the *Turangalîla-Symphonie*.

Mahlermania

When Gustav Mahler died in 1911, his works were not too popular. Luckily, the unceasing efforts of a handful of conductors and musicologists helped to prevent his ten symphonies, his *Das Lied von der Erde* ('Song of the Earth'), and other orchestral songs disappearing from the repertoire. From the 1960s, more orchestras began to feature Mahler's works in concerts and recordings. In turn, the number of Mahler fans began to soar. But real global Mahlermania only started gaining momentum in the 1990s. How closely has HK Phil been associated with this iconic composer?

In the 1970s, Mahler was a rather unfamiliar name to the local audience. HK Phil's first professional season in January 1975 was due to include Mahler's Symphony no. 4, but unforeseen circumstances prevented this. HK Phil's first Mahler performance was in 1977, also Symphony no. 4. Its finale (with its depiction of heaven) was fitting considering it was staged around Easter that year; and the heavenly pleasure in the last movement was interpreted by soprano Ella Kiang. On 11 and 12 August 1978, mezzo-soprano Joann Grillo introduced Mahler's *Lieder eines fahrenden Gesellen* ('Songs of a Wayfarer') to Hong Kong's music-lovers. In the same concert, they were also treated to the 'modern' composer Arnold Schoenberg's *Five Pieces for Orchestra.*

Photo 2.5: Mahler's *Lieder eines fahrenden Gesellen* sung by Sergei Leiferkus. The second half of the concert was Mahler's Symphony no. 7, which garnered a remark by *South China Morning Post*'s Sam Olluver, 'Mahler's majesty is de Waart's triumph.'

Another grand symphony, Anton Bruckner's no. 4, came on 7 and 8 October that year. That may have been HK Phil's first attempt at playing a work by this legendary symphonist.

Works by the three aforementioned composers were programmed by the Principal Conductor and Music Director at the time, Hans Günter Mommer. His bravery in performing these works was remarkable.

Since those times, HK Phil has played Mahler frequently. Edo de Waart is a notable Mahler specialist. From 2004 to 2012, when he was the orchestra's seventh artistic director and principal conductor, his plan was to complete the Mahler symphonic cycle. As it turned out, no. 8, 'Symphony of a Thousand', was the only one left undone.

Photo 2.6: Poster for the Mahler's Symphony no. 7 concert in 2007.

Wish List

Over time, the orchestra has played countless works, big and small, of numerous different genres. However, there are still many great works that deserve to have their HK Phil premieres. Mahler's *Das klagende Lied* ('Song of Lamentation') and Schoenberg's gigantic *Gurre-Lieder* are on the wish lists of veteran music-lovers. The 2024/25 season opened with the orchestra's first performance of Bruckner's Symphony no. 9, conducted by Tarmo Peltokoski. A few of the Austrian composer's early symphonies are also yet to appear on HK Phil's concert platform.

Do you have a wish list too?

Photo 2.7 and Photo 2.8: Under the baton of Music Director Designate Tarmo Peltokoski, HK Phil gave their first performance of Bruckner's Symphony no. 9 to open its 2024/25 season.

3 *Exploring the Storeroom*

Needless to say, the players are HK Phil's treasures. Other treasures – albeit inanimate ones – can be found in the orchestra's storerooms.

HK Phil has been professional for more than half a century. It takes three storerooms to keep its vast collection of instruments. In its early professional days, the orchestra did not even own a harp. During each rehearsal and performance, the orchestra had to borrow the instrument from the City Hall. Things are different now!

Five Sets of Timpani

Most professional orchestras have big instruments such as celestas, bass drums, marimbas, and timpani. The HK Phil is no exception. For timpani alone they have five sets, including a baroque set that is tuned by screws instead of pedals.

The Phil also has two pairs of rotary valve trumpets (in C and B flat), which are often used to play Austro-German works. The player holds the trumpet with two hands side by side. Its sound is more mellow than that of the piston trumpet, making it blend more easily with other instruments. According to Co-Principal Trumpet Christopher Moyse, the rotary valve trumpets are less frequently used in Mahler's symphonies, but under the direction of Tarmo Peltokoski, HK Phil gave it a go to close the 2023/24 season. That Mahler no. 5 had a different sound.

Some instruments are rarely used but are nevertheless indispensable. Mozart's Serenade in B flat major, K. 361, 'Gran Partita', for instance, has two parts written for the basset horn – a single-reed instrument like the clarinet, but with a lower range.

The flugelhorn is like a chubby trumpet with a more fluid sound. It often appears in military and jazz bands. The third movement of Mahler's Symphony no. 3 has a pastoral section. The composer wrote in the score *'Wie die Weise eines Posthorns'*, meaning to play in the way of a posthorn. He did not specify which instrument should be used. In the olden days, the posthorn was played by a postman, sometimes to signal villagers of the arrival of a post rider. In three of the Phil's presentations of the work, the flugelhorn was used to play the passage.

Wagner Tuba

In the mid-nineteenth century, after visiting some factories which produced musical instruments, Richard Wagner decided to have a tuba tailor-made for his *Ring* cycle. He did so to fill the gap between the horns and trombones, creating a noble tone colour to depict Valhalla, where the gods dwell.

Before HK Phil had their own sets of Wagner tubas, the horn would sometimes be used as a substitute (as in the 1983 premiere of *The*

Photo 3.1: In 2018, HK Phil Co-Principal Horn Russell Bonifede gave a public demonstration on how to play the Wagner tuba.

Rite of Spring). When more resources were available, the orchestra would fly in players and their instruments to take part in performances that involved the Wagner tuba. Gradually the instrument became more frequently used, and the orchestra's Ladies' Committee decided to donate a set (which cost around HK$300,000) to the Phil. The four parts of Wagner's *Ring* cycle were performed from 2015 to 2018. In support of this major premiere, some music-lovers bought another set and loaned it to HK Phil. Today, the orchestra has eight Wagner tubas. The Phil also has a bass trumpet and a contrabass trombone, both used in the *Ring*.

Infrequent Visitors

There are some other infrequent 'visitors' to the stage. For example, HK Phil has used two sets of tuned cowbells just once as melodic instruments, for a piece by Joe Hisaishi.

Photo 3.2: On the left are tubular bells normally found in a concert; the two on the right are HK Phil's jumbo collection.

Crotales or antique cymbals are small gongs heard in Claude Debussy's *Prélude à l'après-midi d'un faune* ('Prelude to the Afternoon of a Faun'). HK Phil owns a special set that has a pedal mechanism.

Tubular bells also appear. In addition to the typical ones, HK Phil has a set with longer, lower-sounding tubes. At the 2023 Hong Kong Arts Festival, Unsuk Chin's *Le Chant des enfants des étoiles* ('The Song of the Children of the Stars') called for it. The petite Sophia Woo had to use a stool to reach it!

Made in Hong Kong

HK Phil's most unique treasures were not just 'Made in Hong Kong', but literally home-made and one-of-a-kind.

In the fourth movement of Mahler's Symphony no. 6, there are two or three (or even up to five) 'hammer blows' which denote the mighty blows of fate. The composer did not specify how these strokes were to be produced. On 5 and 6 December 2003, Carlo Rizzi conducted the work. For that occasion, percussionist Raymond Leung designed and produced a huge box and a gigantic hammer. At the concert, its aural and visual effects were equally unforgettable.

On 16 and 17 November 2007, Edo de Waart conducted the orchestra in further performances of the piece. The 'instrument' had more opportunities to shine. It appears we have always had strong hammer players. After having been used four times (not counting the numerous rehearsals), the box is cracked. It may not be able to join the next show: it looks like the blows of fate have overpowered the poor box.

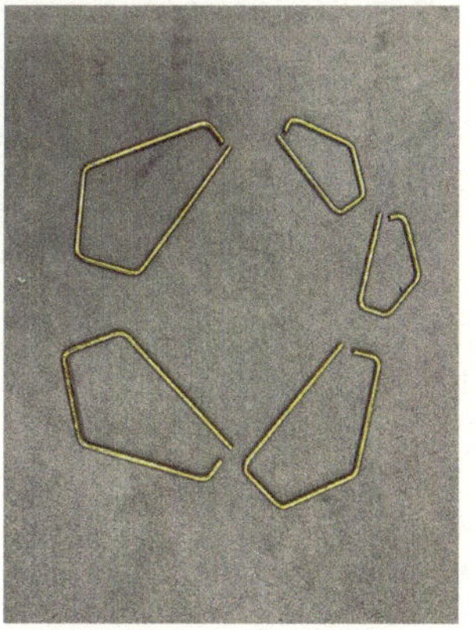

Photo 3.3: Special pentatonic 'triangles'.

The Player Who Calls for Wind and Rain

Raymond Leung is spokesperson of an English instrument-maker. Not long ago, he ordered some pentatonic (non-equilateral) 'triangles' from the company (and yes, this description is confusing; we could just call this instrument a 'pentagon'). These quirky instruments made their debuts at the concert on 22 November 2024 when Angus Lee's . . . *aux cendres* was given its world premiere. Because the instruments have five sides, the patterns of harmonics they generate are quite different from those of conventional triangles. Prior to this, Raymond has also hand-made a wind machine, a few longer-than-normal rain sticks to lengthen the raining sound, and a zinc-plated device to simulate the sound of thunder. Apparently, Raymond can control the weather.

Photo 3.4: HK Phil percussionist Raymond Leung.

Precious Collections

Some HK Phil collections are quite valuable. In the finale of Berlioz's *Symphonie fantastique*, before the solemn *Dies Irae* comes in, we hear the bells. In the past, the notes C and G, were played on the tubular bells. In 2009, HK Phil ordered two real bells that can produce more solid sounds. In the performances on 15 and 16 September 2017, conducted by Long Yu, the bells were backstage and the audience did not see them. The distant sound made it even more spine-chilling.

The bells, which have the orchestra's name engraved on them, appear solid yet gracefully crafted.

Photo 3.5: The HK Phil's custom-made bells featured in the 2019 Jaap | Symphonie Fantastique concert.

Thanks to the support of various parties, the orchestra also has a remarkable line-up of valuable stringed instruments. Some items have been donated, while some are on loan to HK Phil.

Table 3.1: HK Phil stringed instruments as of September 2025

Violin
Giovanni Grancino (*c.* 1715), loaned by the Postscript Collection, played by Wang Liang (second associate concertmaster)
Carlo Antonio Testore (1736), loaned by the Ladies' Committee of the Hong Kong Philharmonic Society
Carlo Antonio Testore (*c.* 1740), loaned by the Postscript Collection, played by Fang Jie (second violin)
Giovanni Battista Guadagnini (*c.* 1760) loaned by the Postscript Collection, played by Jing Wang (concertmaster)[1]
Pietro Giovanni Mantegazza (*c.* 1760), loaned by the Postscript Collection, played by Domas Juškys (co-principal second violin)
Joseph Gagliano (1788), loaned by the Ladies' Committee of the Hong Kong Philharmonic Society, played by Tomoko Tanaka (second violin)
Jean-Baptiste Vuillaume (1866), loaned by the Ladies' Committee of the Hong Kong Philharmonic Society, played by Bei de Gaulle (third associate concertmaster)
Jean-Baptiste Vuillaume (*c.* 1867), loaned by the Postscript Collection, played by Ba Wenjing (first violin)
Enrico Rocca (1902), loaned by the Ladies' Committee of the Hong Kong Philharmonic Society, played by Cheng Li (first violin)
Stefano Scarampella (1905), anonymously loaned, played by Wang Liang (second associate concertmaster)
Ansaldo Poggi (1910), loaned by Laurence Scofield, played by Zhang Xi (first violin)
Riccardo Antoniazzi (1910), loaned by P. C. Woo & Co. played by Leung Kin-fung (first associate concertmaster)[2]

Viola
Lorenzo Storioni (*c.* 1790), loaned by J&A Beares, played by Andrew Ling (principal viola)
Cello
Luigi Fabris (*c.* 1870), loaned by the Stretton Society, played by Fang Xiaomu (co-principal cello)

[1] From 2016 to 2022, Jing Wang played on another renowned violin, a 1760 Giovanni Battista Guadagnini, privately loaned by former Board Director Y. S. Liu.

[2] In addition to this violin, Leung Kin-fung also played on a 1730 Sanctus Seraphin from his personal collection.

As time goes by, wooden instruments mature, and may sound better. This is the case not only for stringed instruments, but also for the xylophone. HK Phil owns a xylophone that was made in the 1950s. It produces a clear and resonant sound. This is, however, not the orchestra's most 'senior' percussion instrument. There is a glockenspiel that is more than one hundred years old! Players like to use it. Its sound is rich and bright, and the audience can hear it even when the whole orchestra is playing loudly.

Photo 3.6: At the 2023 Swire Symphony Under the Stars concert at Central Harbourfront, Richard Bamping played the theme from John Williams's *Schindler's List* on his beautiful Guarneri.

Most players use their own instruments. Richard Bamping's cello was made by Andrea Guarneri in 1674 in Cremona, where many valuable bowed stringed instruments come from. Only nine cellos made by Guarneri are thought to exist now. Next time you hear our principal cellist play a solo passage, close your eyes and be transported to seventeenth-century Italy!

4 *Posting the Posthorn*

HK Phil has programmed Mahler's Symphony no. 3 four times: under Edo de Waart in 2006 and 2010, under Jaap van Zweden in 2016, and under Daniele Gatti in 2025. The special solo passage in the third movement, which the composer indicated should resemble the sound of an old-fashioned postman's horn, was played on the flugelhorn by Principal Trumpet Jonathan Clarke in 2006, by Assistant Principal Trumpet Christopher Moyse, and by Principal Trumpet Nitiphum Bamrungbanthum in 2025. On the third occasion, the Boston Symphony Orchestra's Principal Trumpet Thomas Rolfs served as the postman, personally delivering the scarcely available posthorn from halfway across the globe and playing it for us!

Photo 4.1: This is not a French horn, but rather a posthorn that Thomas Rolfs brought from Boston. Stage Manager Steven Chan is himself a trumpeter, no wonder he took special interest in this obscure brass instrument. Courtesy of Steven Chan.

5 *Playing Out of Sight*

Whether played on the flugelhorn or the posthorn, for the solo in Mahler's Symphony no. 3 the player always plays from backstage, allowing the sound to come through one of the opened stage doors. The composer's intention was to evoke a feeling of distance. To Co-Principal Trumpet Christopher Moyse, it was a surreal experience. He could not see or hear what was happening inside the concert hall, but depended solely on the conductor to achieve a good balance and synchronise with the other instruments. He said, 'Having to wander around backstage for an hour before playing this passage out of sight is more nerve-racking than to stay on stage.'

Photo 5.1: In February 2010, Christopher Moyse was alone backstage at the Cultural Centre, preparing for the performance of Mahler's Third. Though his expression carried a touch of solitude, at least he has his flugelhorn in hand – and photographer Keith Hiro by his side!

6 *An Orchestra 'All Over the Place'*

The places in which SBO and HK Phil have performed reflect the evolution of Hong Kong's performance venues, the orchestra's awareness of the community, and its efforts to expand its audience reach.

Photo 6.1: The Empire Theatre in the 1950s. Courtesy of Haider Kikabhoy.

Question: SBO's trail has led to many different places – except for which of the following?

A. Old City Hall
B. Empire Theatre
C. Loke Yew Hall
D. St. John's Cathedral
E. St. Stephen's Girls' College

The answer is A.

A. The Old City Hall was situated at the site of the present HSBC (The Hongkong and Shanghai Banking Corporation Limited) and Bank of China buildings. Built in 1869, it was demolished completely in 1947: the same year that the SBO came into being.
B. Opened in 1952 in North Point, the Empire Theatre later became the State Theatre. It served as a major performance venue and movie theatre. As of 2025, conservation work is in progress. Among SBO's concerts here was one on 7 December 1954 with Beethoven's Piano Concerto no. 1 in the programme.
C. SBO also performed at the University of Hong Kong's (HKU) Loke Yew Hall. One such performance was Haydn's Creation on 19 March 1956.
D. In the 1950s and 1960s, SBO frequently appeared at St. John's Cathedral, but mainly for rehearsals at the Cathedral's annex. Occasionally, SBO would also rehearse at the Diocesan Boys' School in Kowloon. The school's principal, Gerald Goodban, was one of the SBO's cellists; he offered the orchestra the convenience of rehearsing at the school on condition that students be allowed to spectate. Veteran arts administrator Darwin Chen was one of those student spectators.
E. SBO's first concert took place on 30 April 1948 at St. Stephen Girls' College in the Mid-Levels area of the city. SBO was part of the Sino-British Music Club. The club had put on their first concert (without an orchestra) at the same venue a few months prior, at 9 p.m. on 24 September 1947. There were works for piano solo, vocal solo, and chorus in the programme.

In the years following World War II, with Hong Kong's economy and infrastructure in need of rebuilding, a concert hall was certainly not top priority. In those days, it was not uncommon for concerts to feature the hum of on-stage electric fans – and the noise of outside traffic – as unsolicited 'accompaniment'. A newspaper advertisement for an SBO concert given on 10 June 1954 had this to say: 'Summer has come, shortly we will not have the opportunity to appreciate music.' Set-up on stage was rather primitive. Flip a box over, and there you go – a conductor's podium. The Empire Theatre did not even have a piano; Mr. Donald Fraser of the Education Department was given first-page credit in the concert's programme for letting SBO use his private instrument.

Photo 6.2: SBO performing at the Empire Theatre. Courtesy of the Harry Odell family.

Photo 6.3: HK Phil performing at the Diocesan Boys' School in the 1960s.

Sizeable school halls were used as performance venues. One hotspot on Hong Kong Island was Queen's College; while in Kowloon, the Queen Elizabeth School along with the Diocesan Boys' School frequently provided concert platforms for SBO and (after 1957) HK Phil.

City Hall

When Hong Kong's City Hall was unveiled in March 1962, it showed itself to be a game-changer. Its air-conditioned, well-built, and glorious-sounding concert hall could seat an audience of nearly 1,500 people (a later expansion of the stage decreased this capacity somewhat). The London Philharmonic Orchestra gave five magnificent concerts to mark the hall's opening. Only a month later on 12 April, under the direction of Sir Thomas Armstrong, the pre-professional HK Phil appeared for the first time here, joined with the newly formed combined Christian choir in a performance of Handel's *Messiah*. Both before and after the orchestra turned professional, HK Phil musicians could be heard playing chamber music at the adjacent theatre as well as in the recital hall on the eighth floor of the City Hall's High Block. These performances offered golden opportunities for orchestra members to thrive as all-round musicians, while audiences could appreciate the players' versatility.

In the following three decades, with City Hall's strategic location, Hong Kong Island became the focal point of HK Phil's activities. When rent was not as overwhelming as it later became, the orchestra would rehearse on level eight at the High Block or even inside the Concert Hall. For some years, the Community Hall at Caritas Social Centre in the Mid-Levels was HK Phil's regular rehearsal venue. As a temporary arrangement, percussion players even practiced at a nearby garage on Caine Road.

'Kowloon' Philharmonic

After Hong Kong Baptist College's Academic Community Hall opened in May 1978, the 'Hong Kong' Philharmonic also served as the 'Kowloon' Philharmonic. From August of that year, for three months, Hans Günter Mommer led the orchestra in promotional concerts which showcased popular classics, including concertos with HK Phil players as soloists. From then on, non-residents of Hong Kong Island didn't have to take a ferry or the cross-harbour bus to attend an HK Phil concert.

Photo 6.4: Poster of the Popular Classical Music Concerts in 1978.

'New Territories' Philharmonic

In the 1980s, as Hong Kong's economy took off, more large venues were built. Upon Tsuen Wan Town Hall's inauguration in 1980, HK Phil began to serve as the 'New Territories' Philharmonic. To veterans in the performing arts industry, the Tsuen Wan acoustics are even better than City Hall's. As well as giving concerts there, HK Phil chose to record the album *Colourful Clouds* in Tsuen Wan Town Hall.

In August 1980, Queen Elizabeth Stadium – boasting a 3,000-seat capacity – was opened, and it subsequently came to be a favourite site for HK Phil's large-scale outreach concerts.

An Even Bigger Place

On 3 to 6 September 1982, under the direction of Joseph Koo, HK Phil gave a series of concerts at Queen Elizabeth Stadium, which featured singer Michael Kwan. It was a sensational weekend, a milestone in the history of Hong Kong's Cantopop concerts. In April 1983, the even bigger Hong Kong Coliseum officially opened. HK Phil first performed here in December of that year, along with Liza Wang, Danny Chan, and other stars. In the years that followed, HK Phil frequently came to this bigger place to meet bigger audiences.

Sha Tin and Tuen Mun Town Halls started operations in January and May 1987 respectively, giving music lovers two more concert venues in the New Territories.

The Hong Kong Coliseum is not just an arena for popular classics and popular music. On 1 July 2001, to celebrate the fourth anniversary of the Hong Kong Special Administration Region of the People's Republic of China (HKSAR), Chinese composer Tan Dun led HK Phil in his *Crouching Tiger Concerto* (cello: Felix Fan, *bawu*: Tang Junqiao) and *Water Concerto for Water Percussion and Orchestra* (percussion: David Cossin). On 19 October 2024, another work by Tan Dun received its world premiere at the Coliseum. The piece, *Sound River*, tells the story of the development of human civilisation. The concert featured an enormous performance force, with HK Phil joined by members of the Guangzhou, Macau, and Shenzhen Symphony Orchestras. The venue's vast space was ideal for the staging of such a show. A total of 112 players, seated in the shape of a river in front of a huge screen, created a stately visual impact.

Photo 6.5: Tan Dun's *Sound River* at Hong Kong Coliseum in 2024. Courtesy of LCSD.

Venue Partner

In 1989, the HK Phil moved into the newly opened Hong Kong Cultural Centre. At this venue – the orchestra's present home – there is a 2,000-seat concert hall. Rehearsals always take place on stage. Down in the pit at the 1,700-seat theatre next door, the orchestra has accompanied countless ballets and opera productions. The concert hall's backstage facilities include many dressing rooms and spaces for practice and warm-ups. Players also have their own lockers!

The above is a brief account of venues in which SBO and HK Phil have performed. Orchestral performances usually require a big stage. Large school halls, concert halls, and grand stadiums are obvious choices. Yet the orchestra has shown creative flair in going further to explore unconventional and interesting venues.

7 *Gentle Reminder*

This was the centre page of an HK Phil programme for 19 and 21 March 1971. Note the 'gentle reminder' at the top of the page: 'The acoustics of this Hall are extremely sensitive. Please avoid rustling the paper when reading this Programme.'

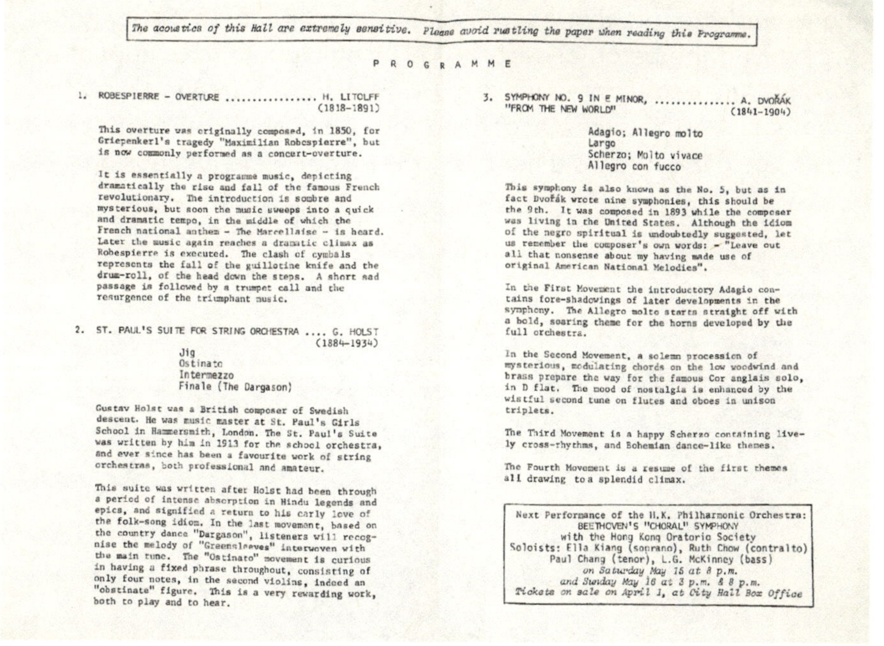

The acoustics of this Hall are extremely sensitive. Please avoid rustling the paper when reading this Programme.

P R O G R A M M E

1. ROBESPIERRE - OVERTURE .... H. LITOLFF (1818-1891)

This overture was originally composed, in 1850, for Griepenkerl's tragedy "Maximilian Robespierre", but is now commonly performed as a concert-overture.

It is essentially a programme music, depicting dramatically the rise and fall of the famous French revolutionary. The introduction is sombre and mysterious, but soon the music sweeps into a quick and dramatic tempo, in the middle of which the French national anthem - The Marcellaise - is heard. Later the music again reaches a dramatic climax as Robespierre is executed. The clash of cymbals represents the fall of the guillotine knife and the drum-roll, of the head down the steps. A short sad passage is followed by a trumpet call and the resurgence of the triumphant music.

2. ST. PAUL'S SUITE FOR STRING ORCHESTRA .... G. HOLST (1884-1934)

Jig
Ostinato
Intermezzo
Finale (The Dargason)

Gustav Holst was a British composer of Swedish descent. He was music master at St. Paul's Girls School in Hammersmith, London. The St. Paul's Suite was written by him in 1913 for the school orchestra, and ever since has been a favourite work of string orchestras, both professional and amateur.

This suite was written after Holst had been through a period of intense absorption in Hindu legends and epics, and signified a return to his early love of the folk-song idiom. In the last movement, based on the country dance "Dargason", listeners will recognise the melody of "Greensleeves" interwoven with the main tune. The "Ostinato" movement is curious in having a fixed phrase throughout, consisting of only four notes, in the second violins, indeed an "obstinate" figure. This is a very rewarding work, both to play and to hear.

3. SYMPHONY NO. 9 IN E MINOR, "FROM THE NEW WORLD" .... A. DVOŘÁK (1841-1904)

Adagio; Allegro molto
Largo
Scherzo; Molto vivace
Allegro con fucco

This symphony is also known as the No. 5, but as in fact Dvořák wrote nine symphonies, this should be the 9th. It was composed in 1893 while the composer was living in the United States. Although the idiom of the negro spiritual is undoubtedly suggested, let us remember the composer's own words: - "Leave out all that nonsense about my having made use of original American National Melodies".

In the First Movement the introductory Adagio contains fore-shadowings of later developments in the symphony. The Allegro molto starts straight off with a bold, soaring theme for the horns developed by the full orchestra.

In the Second Movement, a solemn procession of mysterious, modulating chords on the low woodwind and brass prepare the way for the famous Cor anglais solo, in D flat. The mood of nostalgia is enhanced by the wistful second tune on flutes and oboes in unison triplets.

The Third Movement is a happy Scherzo containing lively cross-rhythms, and Bohemian dance-like themes.

The Fourth Movement is a resume of the first themes all drawing to a splendid climax.

Next Performance of the H.K. Philharmonic Orchestra:
BEETHOVEN'S "CHORAL" SYMPHONY
with the Hong Kong Oratorio Society
Soloists: Ella Kiang (soprano), Ruth Chow (contralto)
Paul Chang (tenor), L.G. McKinney (bass)
on Saturday May 15 at 8 p.m.
and Sunday May 16 at 3 p.m. & 8 p.m.
Tickets on sale on April 1, at City Hall Box Office

Photo 7.1: House programme for the concerts on 19 and 21 March 1971.

8 *Special Sites, Special Shows*

Whether it be up a hill, down underground, or in a shopping mall, park, racecourse, exhibition gallery, Consulate General's residence, or national museum ... HK Phil is everywhere!

It was a particularly freezing day during the orchestra's visit to Beijing in February 1986. Three HK Phil trumpeters in thick coats and gloves were seen playing their instruments on the Great Wall. With them was the orchestra's Music Director, Kenneth Schermerhorn, who waved the baton cheerfully. This iconic photo later appeared on *Musical America*'s cover, making HK Phil known among music lovers overseas. A little secret: according to a creditable source, because it was so cold the three did not really play. They were just posing.

Photo 8.1: Behind this photo is a romantic story. On the day when the picture was taken, Kenneth Schermerhorn proposed to Miss Tish Hooker.

Photo 8.2: In less than a year, the two said their vows at the Cotton Tree Drive Marriage Registry.

Yet HK Phil did play on high ground. One such instance was back in Hong Kong on 10 November 1985: a music walkathon. Along the trail from the Peak to Quarry Bay, musicians gave ensemble performances. While helping to raise fund for the orchestra, they also accompanied hikers with a 'pastoral symphony'.

Hit the High Notes

Photo 8.3: This special helmet has been part of horn player Homer Lee's collection since 2007. Courtesy of Homer Lee.

Another high-ground venue was man-made. What became the skyscraper One Island East was still a building site on 5 November 2007. A HK Phil brass ensemble played Paul Dukas's *La Péri* fanfare at the building's topping-out ceremony. Co-Principal Trumpet Christopher Moyse recalls that his performance attire included a black helmet with HK Phil's 'dragon' logo. At that altitude, the performance literally began and ended on high notes.

Phil Goes Underground

For four consecutive Saturdays from 21 September to 12 October 1991, the HK Phil Brass Quintet appeared inside Hong Kong's Central MTR station. Although the concert's title was 'Phil Goes Underground', there was no 'underground' music at all. Instead, one of the pieces – the main theme from *Star Wars* – launched underground listeners high into space.

Photo 8.4: Poster of Phil Goes Underground.

The above initiatives served the public-relations purpose of bringing the orchestra out of the concert hall. To reach out to potential audiences, HK Phil has also performed in shopping malls such as Taikoo Place, Ocean Terminal, Harbour City, Landmark, New World Centre, and City Plaza.

Photo 8.5 and Photo 8.6: HK Phil × MTR – Phil Your MTR Ride with Music was organised during the COVID pandemic in 2021. Players were filmed making music at Central Station and inside train compartments. Left: Resident Conductor Lio Kuokman and players spent a whole night filming inside Central Station. Right: Associate Principal Bass Clarinet Lorenzo Iosco, who looked like a busker.

Once Upon a Place

An MTR station or a shopping mall can give orchestral performances a local flavour, but venues of historical interest make them nostalgic too. HK Phil has appeared in such places as Tai Kwun (formerly Victoria Prison), Haw Par Mansion, Central Market, and The Mills on the site of the former Nan Fung Cotton Mills.

Photo 8.7: HK Phil × Tai Kwun: Chamber Music Series: The Joy of Bach on 20 June 2022.

Photo 8.8: A masterclass given by pianist Avan Yu held at Haw Par Mansion on 11 September 2022.

Photo 8.9 and Photo 8.10: HK Phil String Quartet appearing in the revitalised Central Market (top) and The Mills (bottom © The Mills).

A Grand Outdoor Performance

HK Phil has performed at other outdoor venues such as Kowloon Park. Nancy Loo vividly remembers playing the *Youth Piano Concerto* (by Liu Shikun, Pan Yiming, Sun Yilin, and Huang Xiaofei) in the park with the pre-professional orchestra under the baton of Lim Kek-tjiang.

In May 2003, Hong Kong was slowly recovering from SARS (severe acute respiratory syndrome). HK Phil's wind ensemble appeared at Hong Kong Park, playing Antonín Dvořák's Serenade in D minor. In December 2021, while the world was in the gloom of COVID-19 (coronavirus disease 2019), the orchestra paid a visit to Hong Kong Disneyland and cheered everyone up!

These were outdoor performances on a relatively small scale. Over the years, HK Phil has also taken part in much bigger promotional events under the sun.

Photo 8.11: The 1979 grand family concert at Sha Tin Racecourse.

On 16 December 1979 (before Queen Elizabeth Stadium and Hong Kong Coliseum were built), HK Phil was the focus of attention at Sha Tin Racecourse. That was an unprecedented family concert attended by more than 10,000 people. Sharing the stage with the orchestra were the Hong Kong Youth Chinese Orchestra and Hong Kong Youth Symphony Orchestra. Renowned singer Roman Tam also made an appearance.

Thirteen years later in 1992, HK Phil was in the spotlight at the racecourse in Happy Valley, taking part in another family concert. This time it was presented by the Urban Council under the title 'Symphony Under the Stars' – which HK Phil adopted as a recurring event. On 1 December 2006, the show was moved to an open space in Hung

Photo 8.12: HK Phil's Principal Patron Swire has been sponsoring the large-scale free outdoor event – Swire Symphony Under the Stars – since 2007. It soon became a tradition for the grand outdoor party to end with Pyotr Il'yich Tchaikovsky's rousing *1812 Overture*, accompanied by fireworks. This picture was taken in 2023. On the podium was Resident Conductor Lio Kuokman.

Hom; it was subsequently relocated back to Happy Valley. For many years, Central Waterfront became the venue of this sought-after event.

Another concert, however, has perhaps drawn the most attention in the orchestra's history. On 30 June 1997, HK Phil appeared on a huge stage at Tamar. At that special moment when Hong Kong's handover took place, the whole world was watching!

When the crowd is not as enormous, the vibe may be totally different . . .

On 30 December 1988, the Hong Kong Convention and Exhibition Centre had just opened. It was here that the orchestra's Ladies Committee organised an extravagant fundraising Viennese Ball. The United Kingdom's Prince and Princess Michael of Kent were invited as honoured guests. Although it was a private party, with the glamour of celebrities, there was another party for the press. Guests danced past midnight to the scintillating music of the Strauss family, played by the orchestra.

Photo 8.13: The Vienna Opera Ball in 1988.
Photo 8.14: Prince and Princess Michael of Kent.

The orchestra has also used the Government House for fundraising dinners. In 2018 and 2021, they gave small-scale performances to audiences that included the chief executive.

Another delightful event took place at the residence of the Consulate General of the Netherlands, where wind players presented Mozart's Serenade in B flat major, 'Gran Partita'. The orchestra has also performed at the Rijksmuseum in Amsterdam, making Dvořák's 'New World' Symphony a 'museum piece'! These two performances were not open to the public.

Love Notes

Another private function took place at Pak Sha Wan Correctional Institution. It was around Christmas, and the audience sang along to Christmas carols. Some players jammed with a band formed by talented inmates.

Photo 8.15: On 15 December 2005, some fifty players became ambassadors for HK Phil at Pak Sha Wan Correctional Institution. Under the direction of Resident Conductor Harmen Cnossen, the orchestra gave two one-hour concerts. Third horn player Homer Lee was the emcee.

HK Phil players in ensembles have visited hospitals and care homes. Music is therapeutic and warms the hearts of patients. On a visit to Bradbury Hospice, the orchestra's Marketing Director Paul Tam wondered how music might benefit patients there. A nurse told him that music touched the caregivers, and in turn they served patients better.

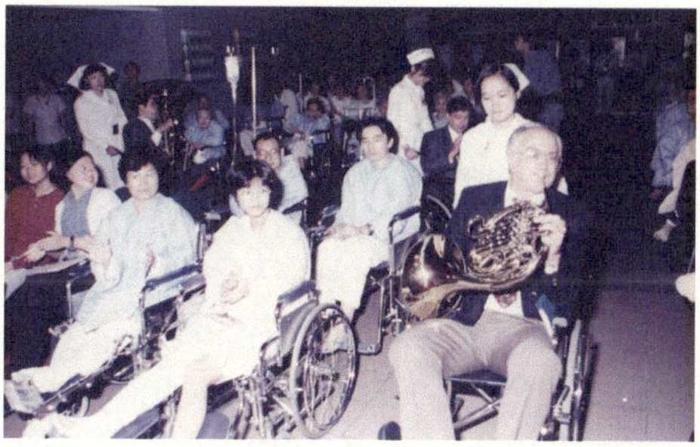

Photo 8.16: Associate Principal Horn Joe Kirtley and colleagues made their entrance in wheelchairs – a wonderful way to kickstart the ensemble's concert at a hospital.

Photo 8.17 and Photo 8.18: On 4 July 2017, HK Phil's string quintet joined a group of Star Wars fanatics 501st Hong Kong Garrison to perform for patients, family members, and medical staff at the Prince of Wales Hospital. This was a part of the Jockey Club Keys to Music Education Programme Ensemble Visit.

That's music for a social cause. In Chapter 20, 'How "Hong Kong" Is the Phil?', there are more stories about how the orchestra actively engages with the community.

9 *Great Hall of the People*

In 1999, David Atherton led the orchestra on a tour of China, which included a concert at the Great Hall of the People in Beijing. Although it has already been more than a quarter of a century, when recalling that special experience of playing there, Principal Clarinet Andrew Simon is still in awe – bear in mind that he is a veteran musician who has performed in countless different venues. That enormous hall has a seating capacity of more than 10,000. It was so big that the notes he played seemed to be travelling far, far away. He describes that unique feeling as 'a thrill of space'!

10 *See You in the Lobby*

At HKCC, the orchestra sometimes plays outside the concert hall. In the 1990s, Resident Conductor Yip Wing-sie led the HK Phil Chorus in free performances at the lobby. Two other occasions of this kind were especially creative, while making effective use of public space.

On 1 and 2 November 2013, an ensemble of players stood at the main staircase, while Lorin Maazel directed Wagner's *Siegfried Idyll*. Audience members crowded around to watch that unique performance. To many, that was a once-in-a-lifetime experience! Why the staircase?

Photo 10.1: Lorin Maazel directed Wagner's *Siegfried Idyll* on the main staircase of the Hong Kong Cultural Centre in 2013.

It was to do with what happened on Christmas Day in 1870. Wagner's wife Cosima (daughter of Franz Liszt) was awoken by some heartwarming music. That was a surprise set up by the composer. Dedicated to his wife, Wagner organised seventeen musicians to play this new piece as a Christmas gift, which was staged at their house's staircase. Cosima was born on Christmas Eve, and her birthdays were usually celebrated on Christmas Day. Their son was eighteen months old then. His name happened to be Siegfried!

On 12 May 2012, the orchestra organised a press conference at the lobby to launch the new season. Towards the end of it, coming from nowhere, Co-Principal Viola Li Bo started meandering among the crowd while plucking his instrument. Then, Principal Flute Megan Sterling came into sight. Slowly, more instruments such as the snare drum and clarinet appeared. Sounds of the trumpet and trombone came from higher floors, as more and more instruments and players (some literally running) gradually joined the party. The music became more exciting, and spectators caught in amazement were busy taking photos and videos. This flash-mob version of Maurice Ravel's *Boléro* is still available for viewing online.

Photo 10.2: HK Phil players performed *Boléro* in the lobby at the 2012/13 season launch press conference.

11 *A Catalogue of Mishaps*

Concerts do not always run smoothly. After all, 'things happen'! Players are fallible like anyone else. What matters most is how one recovers from these incidents.

Photo 11.1 and Photo 11.2: Solomon Bard.

Dr Solomon Bard wrote in his autobiography *Light and Shade* about how he took over the baton from 'an obviously inebriated army bandmaster'. He said, 'It was not until this gentleman had staggered and nearly fallen off the podium, two rehearsals later, that I was invited to replace him and thus become the orchestra's (SBO) first permanent conductor.'

He was invited to a luncheon organised by the Friends of the Philharmonic. A report of that meeting appeared in the February–March 1985 issue of *Upbeat*:

'On one occasion, when I was conducting, the beginning was so ragged and out of tune, that I stopped the orchestra and started again.'

In the early 1960s, a HK Phil timpanist was supposed to come in with a drum roll to begin a movement. The moment came, and Bard was surprised to discover that he was asleep. Probably the sound of the strings in the previous movement had been too soft and tender!

Another timpanist (not the one mentioned above!) suffered from a heart attack before going on stage, and the second trumpet had a motorcycle accident. Nevertheless, the concert went on as scheduled.

Students usually served as ushers for concerts which took place at Loke Yew Hall of HKU. For unknown reasons, one time the ushers did not show up. Players took the youngsters' shifts before stealthily sneaking back onto the stage.

Even the orchestra's professional era saw the occasional slip-up.

Sick on Stage

When sickness (or literally 'sick') appears on stage, it can be really messy. Freelance oboist Leanne Nicholls recalls a concert that happened some twenty odd years ago: 'I found the principal oboist in the dressing room during intermission with her head down. I asked if she was OK.' She had food poisoning after eating oysters. Leanne was on high alert while sitting next to her during the second half, ready to take over her part if she had to dash off. 'The final note was played, but all of a sudden, she vomited. The viola section [in front of her] were more "in the line of fire" than me. I grabbed her oboe and then quickly got her upstairs to get washed and changed.' That oboist was in hospital for a week after that, as the dehydration was serious.

That incident was frightening for Leanne. 'I have never had oysters, and never will after the scene I saw that day!'

A similar incident happened at the Bangkok Pre-tour Concert on 18 October 2023. A clarinettist struggled through the first half before throwing up on stage. The start of the second half was delayed for ten minutes, as the place had to be cleaned up and disinfected. Audience members could smell the strong scent of sanitiser spray! The clarinettist soldiered on despite the discomfort and managed to finish the concert. He was asked by the conductor to stand up to acknowledge the audience's applause. As he left the stage, he vomited again. Luckily, the food-poisoning was not as serious as that of the oboe player mentioned earlier. The next day, after seeing a doctor, he was on time to rejoin the Bangkok tour.

These two cases reflect the innate musician's professionalism and special will-power.

Timely Rescue

The orchestra's personnel manager must respond swiftly when a musician is unwell. More stories from Leanne Nicholls:

As an extra, she once got a call at 11 p.m. to see if she could board a coach at 9 a.m. for a rehearsal at Yuen Long Theatre. The performance took place that evening. That ten-hour notice was generous compared with another case . . .

She was going to bring a conductor friend to a HK Phil concert. Thirty minutes before she left home, the manager asked if she could stand in for a player. Luckily, she still had time to get changed and grab her instrument. That conductor friend never imagined his friend would turn out to be a player on stage. Another time, it was *The Nutcracker*. An oboist had a bad case of the flu and was too frail to play on. During intermission, the manager decided to look for a replacement. It was another narrow escape, as Leanne was teaching near the Cultural Centre, and happened to be wearing black. In no time, she found herself sight-reading the ballet in the pit.

When a player is sick, there may still be time to look for a substitute musician. However, something absolutely 'on-the-spot' can happen too!

Break a Leg, Break a String

Photo 11.3: Jaap van Zweden and Nicola Benedetti.

Most string players have experienced a broken string while on stage. If it happens with a single tutti player, the worst that happens is that they have to stop while others play on. If a soloist's string breaks, however, that is another story. The first time Yo-Yo Ma played with the orchestra in December 1986, one of his strings broke during the finale of the Shostakovich Cello Concerto no. 1. The performance came to a halt! The audience had to wait for him to replace a string and return from backstage. On 7 February 2013, it was the case of Nicola Benedetti's violin. A string broke at the beginning of the Tchaikovsky Violin Concerto.

On 5 May 2023, HK Phil was premiering Elliot Leung's Symphony no. 1, 'The Metaverse'. It was the turn of Jian Wang's instrument while the concertmaster was playing his solo. Second Associate Concertmaster Anders Hui immediately handed his violin over to Jian to let him continue, while he quickly replaced the string in full view of the audience. The experience of another Second Associate Concertmaster, Wang Liang, was inspiring. When the E-string on his violin broke, his reflex action was to keep going, playing at higher positions on the A-string. The hours he had spent practising higher positions paid off at that moment.

A Musician's Crisis Awareness

Musicians are full of crisis awareness. Some violinists put extra strings inside the pocket of their concert dress. Wind players like to keep a box of extra reeds on stage. You never know when one of those reeds may become your lifesaver. Percussionists have extra mallets. However, the extra gear may not always be on hand.

As percussionist Sophia Woo played in a performance, the head of one of her hammers flew off. Thankfully, it did not hit anyone (her sweetheart – Homer Lee, who played the third horn – was sitting in front of her). Sophia immediately sneaked backstage to look for an extra hammer. Her quick thinking was impressive. She was soon back at her position, not missing a beat!

As for conductors, dropping the baton is not out of the ordinary. I once saw a viola player pick up a baton for the maestro, who responded with a smile. One cannot be sure, however, where that baton may land. Sometimes, upon a conductor's request, the orchestra's librarian Betty Ho would place a standby baton on the conductor's music stand – hoping, of course, that they won't have to use it!

First Aid Kit

Betty is more than a librarian. She helps solve last-minute problems too. Having gathered substantial experience, she has a stockpile of black socks, shirts, white bow ties, and cufflinks ready at the office. There is a big case in the backstage area where Betty keeps music scores. This also doubles as her 'first aid kit', with things like a sewing bag, safety pins, sticky tape, adhesive bandages, rubber bands, and paracetamol inside!

During a trip to the Chinese mainland in 2019, piano soloist Rachel Cheung was shortly to go on stage. Her mother suddenly realised she had forgotten to bring a hair-clip. While it may look stylish to let your hair loosely fall, Rachel was going to play and conduct at the same time; she needed to have her hair neatly held. Fortunately, Betty recalled seeing an usher backstage who wore a hair-clip, and quickly went to borrow it from her. Betty and the usher both became lifesavers that time!

Years ago, a female player forgot to wear a black top. Because Betty can be seen on stage, she is always in black. Guess whose black blazer that absent-minded player sported that evening?

Betty reminds me of a song:

Winter, spring, summer or fall
All you have to do is call
And I'll be there, yes, I will . . .

Thank you, Betty!

12 *A Hybrid of Absentmindedness and Intelligence*

Two absentminded players solved their own problems!

Once, a player forgot to bring his black shoes to a concert and kept his colourful gym shoes on. As a solution, that player took off his socks (which happened to be in black) and wore them outside, literally wrapping his shoes! No one seemed to notice it during the performance!

A one-of-a-kind violinist forgot to bring his instrument to a school concert held at Tsuen Wan Town Hall. It turned out to be another testament of how nimbly the musician's mind moves. There was no time to panic. The player dashed to the crowded lobby, hoping that one of the audience members might have just finished a violin lesson at school. Bingo! there he was – a student with a violin on his back. A few minutes later, the student was watching his instrument make a HK Phil debut! To him, that must have been an interesting feeling: 'Wow! My violin has taken part in a professional performance!'

PS That violinist was not alone: other players have also come to work without their instruments. You might like to call those special cases – 'empty' cases!

13 *A Bang on the Bass*

Most orchestral stringed instruments have four strings pressing down on the bridge. Sometimes the tension may make the bridge slant (usually towards the fingerboard). If this is not noticed by the player, the bridge may fall, and the impact can be heavy. Years ago, this happened with a double bass, and at a quiet moment in a piece! Everyone looked around to see where that 'gunshot' sound had come from. Luckily, the instrument wasn't seriously injured – just a tiny scratch on its soundbox.

14 *Between 1 and 2*

Photo 14.1: Fou Ts'ong collaborated with Principal Guest Conductor Maxim Shostakovich in a concert which featured a Chopin concerto.

It was May 1985. Associate Principal Horn Joe Kirtley knew that Chopin's Piano Concerto no. 1 in E minor would soon be featured in a programme. The piece had some tricky high notes. So, he intensively drilled those passages at home. The orchestral rehearsal went well. He played brilliantly. The soloist would come on Thursday morning . . .

With the soloist ready to play, there came the downbeat from Maxim Shostakovich. After a couple of bars, however, the soloist looked confused. He stood up, waved to the conductor, and called out, 'No! Not no. 1! Should be no. 2!'

This perplexed pianist was Fou Ts'ong.

The rehearsal was suspended as the librarian and other staff members quickly went looking for the music scores of Chopin's F minor

Piano Concerto no. 2. Soon, parts were found and distributed. There had been a miscommunication between Fou Ts'ong and the orchestra office. Joe Kirtley found this dramatic scene unforgettable.

On the day of the concert, there was a separate insertion in the programme to introduce the F minor Piano Concerto no. 2!

15 *The Audience Has Mishaps Too!*

There have been discussions on whether an audience should clap between movements. It is not uncommon to hear audience members clap after the rousing third movement of Tchaikovsky's 'Pathétique' Symphony. What about when the piece is not finished yet? In the same composer's Symphony no. 5, before the coda – when the glorious tutti comes to a short pause – some people are tempted to clap. In fact, there are two more minutes to go. Another hot spot that lures the audience to clap is towards the end of Carl Maria von Weber's *Invitation to the Dance*. Often, the final cello solo has to battle its way against the audience's applause to get heard. A clip of Principal Cello Richard Bamping doing just that can be seen online!

Another classic audience slip-up is to do with the start time of a concert. A normal HK Phil concert starts at 8 p.m.[1] For various reasons, sometimes HK Phil chooses to start earlier, at 7.30 p.m. On 18 October 2023, HK Phil's Bangkok Pre-tour Concert took place at Yuen Long Theatre. Quite a few people arrived late. At 8 p.m., they were watching the show on the TV monitor outside the auditorium. Among audience members who had not taken note of the start time was ME!

1 In SBO's day, a concert might start as late as 9.30 p.m.

16 *Ping-Pong Concerto – Who Wants to Be a Soloist?*

Photo 16.1: Principal Guest Conductor Long Yu directed the orchestra in Swire Denim Series and Swire Sunday Family Series: Ping Pong Diplomacy, 9–11 June 2017.

Hong Kong's special geographical location and openness to the outside world, coupled with our highly innovative spirit, have attracted artists with many different talents to the stage with our orchestra. Here is a glimpse of some of our more unusual collaborators.

East Meets West

Chinese instruments seldom appear in a Western orchestra. Cultural differences may be a factor. Hong Kong, though, is a place where East meets West, and quite a few Chinese instruments have shone on HK Phil's concert platform. In 2009, Guo Yazhi collaborated with the orchestra, playing on the *suona* and *guanzi* in *Trackers of Yellow River* and *A Hundred Birds Paying Tribute to the Phoenix* respectively. In a baroque concert in 1984, Ku Hui-man was *pipa* soloist in a Vivaldi concerto originally written for the lute. Likewise, Xu Ke played Vittorio Monti's *Csárdás* on the *erhu* in 2003.

Whenever the *Yellow River Piano Concerto* is played, the *dizi* can be heard. At the 2023 National Day Concert, there was a special Hong Kong premiere of Zhao Lin's *A Thousand Li of Rivers and Mountains*. A Chinese instrument (or a singer) was featured in each movement, played respectively by guest soloists Wei Shen-fu (*sheng*), Zhang Ying (*pipa*), Xu Hui (*erhu*), and Wu Chih-ting (*dizi*) – all members of the Hong Kong Chinese Orchestra.

Photo 16.2: Principal Guest Conductor Long Yu and members of the Hong Kong Chinese Orchestra in National Day Concert: A Panorama of Rivers and Mountains, 2023.

HK Phil has also embraced Chinese vocal music traditions. A *qingyi* (the main female role in Chinese operas) joined the Hong Kong premiere of Chen Qigang's *Iris dévoilée*. Meng Meng sang this intriguing part and also took the second soprano role.

Super-high Soprano

Sopranos are regularly featured as soloists in HK Phil's concerts, but it is rare for the voice part to be treated as an 'instrument'. Reinhold Glierè wrote a concerto for coloratura soprano and orchestra. Beverly Hoch joined the orchestra to record this work in 1986. On 3 and 4 January in the same year she first appeared as soloist in a concert at City Hall, singing the challenging Air and Variations for soprano and orchestra by Heinrich Proch. There is a top A flat in the score. It may have been the highest note ever sung in a HK Phil concert. Incidentally, *hoch* is the German word for 'high'.

Alternative Soloists

Many other off-the-beaten-track concertos have appeared in HK Phil's programmes. These are not necessarily contemporary works – in fact, Schumann's Konzertstück in F major for four horns and orchestra is seldom heard. On 2 and 3 June 2023, two members of German Hornsound partnered with HK Phil's own Lin Jiang and Russell Bonifede to present the work. Although there was a moderately sized audience, the response was enthusiastic.

Photo 16.3: Anja Bihlmaier directed the orchestra joined by (from left) Timo Steininger, Russell Bonifede, Christoph Eß, and Lin Jiang in Schumann's Konzertstück in F major.

The double bass is almost indispensable in orchestral music. Yet the instrument is seldom featured in solos. Renowned bassist Gary Karr has been HK Phil's soloist on different occasions. The concerts on 3 and 4 June 1983 were double delights, with Karr playing Domenico Dragonetti's Double Bass Concerto in A major[1] and Niccolò Paganini's 'Moses' Fantasy. HK Phil's first PR manager, Cynthia Hydes, once helped look after Karr. She said he was a great comedian who brought the house down with his wit.

Photo 16.4: Gary Karr.

The Lowest Brass and the Highest Woodwind

In an orchestra's brass section, the instrument with the lowest range is the tuba. On 25 and 27 October, Principal Tuba Paul Luxenburg, who had been with HK Phil for less than two months, was soloist in the tuba concerto written by John Williams. The contrabassoon is even lower; on 2 December 1978, it became the protagonist in a piece entitled *Leviathan* by Ruth Gipps. In the same concert, the audience was treated to other concertos that put the piccolo, cor anglais, harmonica, and double bass in the limelight. This interesting programme was curated by conductor Hans Günter Mommer.

[1] It has been asserted that Édouard Nanny attributed the piece to himself.

A Drum Installation

Likewise, the timpani are hardly seen as solo instruments. Principal Timpani James Boznos, however, has been featured at least three times as the orchestra's soloist. On 20 and 21 April 2007, audience members were amazed by what they saw on stage. It was an ensemble of kettledrums of different sizes meticulously set up in a rounded formation, literally encircling the soloist!

Photo 16.5: Principal Timpani James Boznos and his 'circle of friends'!

Daiko

Even larger than the timpani is the *daiko*. On 27 and 28 September 2006, Eitetsu Hayashi shared the stage with HK Phil, giving a passionate rendition of *Fujin-Raijin* ('The Gods of Wind and Thunder') by Tokuhide Niimi. This called for the Cultural Centre pipe-organ to be used. It was a stormy concert indeed!

Photo 16.6: Eitetsu Hayashi with HK Phil.

When a percussion concerto is performed, the audience is always intrigued by the variety of sound effects. More than that, since the instruments and the players are placed at the front, instead of their usual position in the back, the visual effect is splendid too. HK Phil has programmed quite a few percussion concertos. Andy Akiho's *Ricochet*: Triple Concerto for Ping-Pong, Violin and Percussion with Orchestra, may be the most unconventional. It is a work with theatrical elements. Percussionist David Cossin was joined by violinist Kristin Lee along with professional table tennis players Ariel Hsing and Michael Landers, who were 'playing' both musically and athletically on stage. It was so much fun!

What Is an Instrument?

What other unorthodox instruments have appeared on HK Phil's concert stage? Let me name a few: the titular typewriter in Leroy Anderson's piece; paper (including sounds deliberately made by turning pages), water, and pebbles used in works by Tan Dun; and the huge box and hammer in Mahler's Symphony no. 6, as mentioned in the chapter 'Exploring the Storeroom'.

Looking to the future, I have longed to see and hear Tchaikovsky's *1812 Overture* with genuine cannons! In previous performances, those powerful blasts were usually simulated by the bass drum or synthesizer. It would be exciting to see real cannons on stage – in an outdoor setting, of course.

17 *The Different Cimbalom*

Zoltán Kodály's *Háry János* suite was in the programme of a HK Phil concert in the 1970s. Its score calls for the obscure cimbalom. Even today, it would be difficult to procure a cimbalom in Hong Kong – let alone back then, when resources were scarce.

The super-creative David Gwilt was the pianist for the concert. He came up with a solution. He first wrapped two lengths of wood loosely with tin foil. Then he placed them on top of the strings inside the soundbox of the grand piano, covering the whole range used in the cimbalom part. During the performance, audience members heard metallic, string-beating sounds. Yet not a dulcimer, *yangqin* or cimbalom was seen on stage.

Contemporary composer John Cage is noted for placing screws and erasers, among other objects, inside the piano's soundbox. David Gwilt's performance in *Háry János* may be the first time the HK Phil used such 'prepared piano' techniques.

18 *Made for Each Other*

A symphony orchestra runs the gamut of tone colours, dynamics, textures, range and in turn, emotions. No wonder it makes an ideal partner for different art forms, generating much synergy.

A Model of Multi-media

In November 2002, the closing programme of Hong Kong's New Vision Arts Festival was Mahler's *Das Lied von der Erde*. The performance brought together the orchestra (chamber orchestra version by Schoenberg/Riehn), the voice, dance, poetry, and the visual arts. HK Phil was joined by contralto Ulrika Tenstam, tenor Warren Mok, conductor Kerstin Nerbe, and the Hong Kong Dance Company.

When working on *The Song of the Earth*, Mahler was inspired by translated Tang dynasty poems. Contemporary poet Cheng Chou-yu reworked the German lyrics, and the revised Chinese version was narrated by actor Lisa Yan Lu. The stage displayed four paintings created by Chuang Che. Chiang Ching was the director, choreographer, and set and props designer. The final product was an amalgamation of performing arts (music, dance and narration), visual arts (painting), and literary arts (poetry). Of course, there were also the essential elements of theatrical arts such as lighting and set design.

It was a rare opportunity for HK Phil to be involved with a multimedia production to such an extent. There are, however, countless examples of the orchestra collaborating with other art forms and performance mediums. The most obvious example is opera, which by nature is multi-media.

Opera

'Father of Hong Kong Opera' Lo King-man's first production included highlights from four operas (with piano accompaniment by So Hau-leung, who incidentally became the professional HK Phil's first General Manager in 1974). Lo first collaborated with an orchestra in 1968 for a production of Gaetano Donizetti's *L'elisir d'amore* with the pre-professional HK Phil, conducted by Arrigo Foa. Lim Kek-tjiang conducted Giuseppe Verdi's *La Traviata* with HK Phil in 1969. When Hans Günther Mommer was HK Phil's Music Director, Lo King-man had an even closer relationship with the orchestra, staging Giacomo Puccini's *Madama Butterfly* (1977) and *Tosca* (1978) and the double-billed Pietro Mascagni's *Cavalleria rusticana* and Ruggero Leoncavallo's *Pagliacci* (1979). Carl Pini was made HK Phil's concertmaster and assistant conductor in 1980, and in March 1981 he conducted Donizetti's *Don Pasquale*.

Photo 18.1 (left): Programme of HK Phil's first opera production, *L'elisir d'amore*. Courtesy of Walter Wong.
Photo 18.2 (rIght): Soprano Ella Kiang in the title role of *Madame Butterfly*. Courtesy of Kathy Lam.

In the early 1980s, mezzo-soprano Joann Grillo was instrumental in bringing singers from New York's Metropolitan Opera to Hong Kong during the Met's summer breaks. It was highlights of arias in 1981. The following year, scenes from four operas were showcased. In 1983, full productions of *Madama Butterfly* and Georges Bizet's *Carmen*, with Metropolitan singers in the lead, were put on stage. HK Phil provided accompaniment for those and many subsequent opera performances. Some memorable ones include the Hong Kong Arts Festival's productions of Tan Dun's *Marco Polo* and Richard Strauss's *Der Rosenkavalier* and *Salome*.

The orchestra broke new ground in opera shortly after Edo de Waart assumed his post as Artistic Director and Chief Conductor in 2004. He introduced an 'opera in concert' initiative. Among others, Beethoven's *Fidelio* and the rarely performed *Elektra* by Richard Strauss were presented. In HK Phil's fiftieth professional season, Jaap van Zweden directed a concert version of Wagner's *Der fliegende Holländer* ('The Flying Dutchman') to great acclaim. It was the Dutch conductor's last season with HK Phil as its music director.

The orchestra collaborates regularly with Opera Hong Kong. Recent productions included *La Traviata* (2022), *Tosca* (2023), and *Turandot* to mark the hundredth anniversary of the death of Puccini in 2024.

The Ring in the Pit

During the 20th Beijing Music Festival in October 2017, HK Phil performed Wagner's *Die Walküre* in the late maestro Herbert von Karajan's 'Salzburg version'. For the first time, the orchestra was in the pit to play part of the *Ring*. First Associate Concertmaster Leung Kin-fung recalls the experience of being squeezed into the pit at Poly Theatre with eighty-six other players. The place only fit two harps (in the concert version in Hong Kong, there were six!) It was the most 'intimate' setting!

Once in his position, the conductor Jaap van Zweden could in no way leave the pit during the performance. String players had to be careful not to let their bows poke their colleagues.

Ballet

HK Phil has joined Hong Kong Ballet for innumerable performances of *The Nutcracker* over the years. From 1988 to 2000, Yip Wing-sie was HK Phil's resident conductor and directed most of the annual performances of the Christmas favourite, except for one or two years when she was pregnant. The orchestra has also taken part, multiple times, in other favourite ballets such as Sergei Prokofiev's *Romeo and Juliet*, Tchaikovsky's *Swan Lake*, and Adolphe Adam's *Giselle*, among others.

Aside from the standard ballet repertoire, the orchestra has been involved in various contemporary productions. From 14 to 16 October 2022, Hong Kong Ballet staged an adventurous *Carmina Burana*. The orchestra was in the pit. On stage, there were three big structures erected in a U-shape, with choir members standing on three tiers. Hanging in the middle was a 'wheel of fortune'. This perfectly set the scene for Carl Orff's music and for the movements choreographed by Septime Webre. Within six months, from 23 to 26 March 2023, the two organisations joined forces again in another refreshing production – the world premiere of Peter Salem's *Coco Chanel: The Life of a Fashion Icon*.

Photo 18.3: A grand production of *Carmina Burana* co-presented by HK Phil and Hong Kong Ballet in 2022.

Drama

Photo 18.4: Poster of the 2001 Magic Circle Mime Music, Noise and Silence concert.

In addition to opera and dance, the orchestra has featured drama on stage too. The Magic Circle Mime Co. from the United States was a regular collaborator. Since the 1990s the company's two lead artists, Maggie Petersen and Douglas MacIntyre, have brought a number of programmes to HK Phil. Many children who watched the first of those family shows are parents now.

From 20 to 22 January 1989, the HK Phil Chorus was featured in a programme entitled Opera Extravaganza at Queen Elizabeth Stadium, featuring famous opera choruses. Two actors, Wong Ho Yi and Chan Tsing, wore costumes and makeup to play the two featured composers, Wagner and Verdi. It was visually impressive – and as they bantered with each other, audience members subtly came to know more about the two Romantic masters.

Star Conductors

The first Symphony Under the Stars concert took place at Happy Valley Sports Ground in 1992. One highlight was Jackie Chan featuring as a 'guess' conductor – literally guessing where those strong beats, cues, and cut-offs were! He led the orchestra in the final part of Gioachino Rossini's *William Tell* Overture. During rehearsal, Jackie asked the players not to watch him too often, lest the music fall apart! At the show, upon his request, the genuine conductor Yip Wing-sie sat on stage so that Jackie could see her and mimic her movements. It turned out to be a 'safe landing'.

On the same occasion, another entertainment icon, Eric Tsang Chi-wai, also became a one-off maestro. Wing-sie said he was very talented. She demonstrated to him only once how to conduct Nicolai Rimsky-Korsakov's *Flight of the Bumble Bee*. Immediately, Eric was able to do it perfectly and wittily. Instead of a baton in his hand, he used a fly-swatter – an unusual tool to deal with a bumble bee!

From Movie Stars to the Cinema

From time to time the orchestra features movie music, paying tribute to film scorers such as John Williams (27–28 January 2012) and Hans Zimmer (5–6 January 2024). There have also been performances featuring a wide range of musicals, for example 'Rodgers & Hammerstein on Stage and Screen' (12–13 February 2016). Excerpts of such classic movies as *Oklahoma*, *Carousel*, *South Pacific*, and *The King and I* were shown onscreen, while their iconic tunes were played live.

'Movies in Concert' is another of HK Phil's initiatives. The idea is to show the whole film in the concert hall while the orchestra plays the accompanying music. One might ask, 'Why not just play the movie with the original audio dubbing, perfectly synchronised?' Well, in terms of accuracy, a carefully administered studio production has an edge over a live orchestra. However, the unamplified live concert sound, with natural acoustics, played along with a movie, is its own form of art.

Whether action movies such as *Star Wars* or *Raiders of the Lost Ark*, science fiction such as *Jurassic Park*, or Broadway blockbusters such as *West Side Story*, cinema-lovers and music-lovers alike simply loved them. An audience member Tin Wing-sin recalls, 'It was fascinating.

Marni Nixon's golden voice was accompanied live by HK Phil; and in the special ambience of a concert hall. The feel is beyond compare!'

This special art form has another edge: when compared with the olden days, cinemas are getting smaller now. There are not many chances left to enjoy a movie with a big crowd, inside a huge venue!

On 3 January 2025 it was the turn of Swire Denim Series to feature a movie, with *Crouching Tiger, Hidden Dragon* Live in Concert. Before the movie was shown, conductor Benjamin Northey told everyone that Tan Dun was actually in the audience. A big round of applause immediately followed as Tan stood up and waved to everyone. It was a unique experience to be in the same house with the composer, enjoying the work that won him an Academy Award for Best Original Score!

The presence of a live orchestra 'accompanying' *Crouching Tiger* enabled one to experience an intimate feel of the colourful instrumentation: the meandering strings, beautiful solo cello, intriguing *pipa*, and exotic *bawu*. When it came to the sword-fighting scenes, the percussion section delivered sounds that had far more depth than those coming out of the speakers of a conventional cinema.

Photo 18.5: Swire Denim Series: *Crouching Tiger, Hidden Dragon* Live in Concert in 2025.

2014 marked the 125th anniversary of the birth of Charlie Chaplin. It has also been one hundred years since the legendary comic actor created his iconic character, the Tramp (in *Kid Auto Races at Venice*). From 2 to 5 May, *City Lights* (with music composed by Charlie Chaplin) and *Kid Auto Races at Venice* were shown at commemorative concerts. I find silent movies in concert closest to the original, and the most perfect match. After all, back in those days, sometimes there was a pianist or a small accompanying ensemble in the cinema. Here at Cultural Centre, the mission was accomplished by a full orchestra; and because there was no dialogue, loudspeakers were left idle!

Photo 18.6: Tan Dun was watching the movie and listening to the HK Phil at the same time! Audience members clapped non-stop when his name appeared in the credits. Another thunderous round of applause followed when he later took to the stage.

The Earth's Musical Journey

Another sought-after genre is the screening of documentaries. From 2015, Hong Kong audience experienced major BBC productions including *Blue Planet*, *Planet Earth*, and *Frozen Planet* at Cultural Centre Concert Hall accompanied by original music played by the orchestra. From the towering peaks of Nepal to the lush green of the Amazon, from iceberg-filled oceans to brightly coloured coral reefs, audiences were treated to spectacular audio and visual discoveries.

Boléro on Sand

Audiovisual enjoyment was part of the fun at the 2015 Swire Symphony Under the Stars too. Local sand painting artist Hoi Chiu created amazing images on big screens as the orchestra played Ravel's *Boléro*.

Photo 18.7 and Photo 18.8: Sand painting artist Hoi Chiu was HK Phil's stage partner at the 2015 Swire Symphony Under the Stars.

Magic

The emcee for the evening happened to be the magician Harry Wong. On numerous occasions, he greeted audiences with his distinctive tricks. He never made a conductor or players vanish, though.

Photo 18.9: Harry Wong and the HK Phil bass section.

Cirque de la Symphonie

From 11 to 13 May 2018, gigantic metal scaffolds were seen on stage at Cultural Centre Concert Hall. It was HK Phil's collaboration with Cirque de la Symphonie, which brought much excitement and charm with fascinating acts by acrobats, jugglers, weight-lifters, dancers, and contortionists. Considering its synchronisation with the music, one couldn't help but think that Tchaikovsky might have composed his pieces especially for these acts!

Photo 18.10: Swire Denim Series: Cirque de la Symphonie.

The Art of Speech

Sometimes, the orchestra's concerts have voiceovers and narration. During their first professional season, HK Phil included a performance of Prokofiev's *Peter and the Wolf* with Cantonese narration. It was also common in those days for the orchestra to programme Britten's *The Young Person's Guide to the Orchestra* in a narrated version at school concerts.

Photo 18.11, Photo 18.12, and Photo 18.13: At a school concert organised as part of the 2018 Jockey Club Keys to Music Education Programme where *Peter and the Wolf* was performed; it was quite obvious which instrument was representing which character.

Here Comes the Consul General

It was a full American programme on 20 and 21 April 2007. Most fittingly, the orchestra invited James B. Cunningham, then Consul General of the United States of America in Hong Kong, to be narrator of Aaron Copland's *Lincoln Portrait*.

Photo 18.14: Under the baton of Xian Zhang, HK Phil shared the stage with James B. Cunningham, the then Consul General of the United States of America in Hong Kong.

One other collaborator was a diva – as you'll read in the next chapter . . .

19 *The Diva*

The multiple-award-winning Sylvia Chang was in the spotlight with HK Phil on 3 and 4 November 2023. The versatile scriptwriter, director and actress assumed the role of a narrator this time. She displayed her remarkable talent by portraying fourteen roles in an adaptation of Shakespeare's *A Midsummer Night's Dream* by Taiwanese writer Chiao Yuan-pu. Characters such as the mischievous Puck, the steadfast lover Helena, the graceful Queen of the Fairies, and the ridiculous Bottom were played most convincingly. On top of that, Sylvia was an eloquent storyteller. Coupled with Felix Mendelssohn's beautiful music, it was an enchanting experience.

It was not the diva's first collaboration with HK Phil. In 1991, her name was among a list of singers at a pop concert presented by the orchestra at Hong Kong Coliseum.

Photo 19.1: *A Midsummer's Night's Dream* with Sylvia Chang.

20 *How 'Hong Kong' Is the Phil?*

The orchestra's activities mainly take place in Hong Kong, situated in Southern China. Audience members are mostly Hong Kong people. Aside from these geographical and clientele considerations, being named a 'Hong Kong' orchestra has a lot more implications.

Sinfonia Domestica

Since the handover of Hong Kong, HK Phil's recording of the national anthem has been played repeatedly on radio and TV. Most Hong Kong people have indeed become HK Phil's listeners without noticing it! In this regard, Hong Kong is literally a domestic orchestra.

More than that, in my opinion, HK Phil is closely linked with Hong Kong in at least three ways.

1. It Belongs to Hong Kong

At many 'official' occasions, we see the name Hong Kong Philharmonic Orchestra.

Festival of Hong Kong

On Hong Kong Memory, a multi-media website, is this description: 'The Hong Kong government held three Hong Kong Festivals in 1969, 1971 and 1973, with the intention that through different forms of participation in a wide variety of activities – large-scale and small-scale, indoors and outdoors – the people in Hong Kong might develop a sense of belonging and identity.' HK Phil took part each time. On 8 December 1969, under the direction of Lim Kek-tjiang, the orchestra gave a concert with many Hong Kong elements in it. *Festival of Hong Kong Fanfare* by William

Lovelock (a frequent visitor to Hong Kong whose series of music theory books were extensively used by Hong Kong students) opened the programme. It was followed by the work of another English composer, Malcolm Arnold's *Hong Kong Anniversary Overture* (a piece commissioned by HK Phil and premiered in 1968; see Chapter 43). Then came a 'festival suite', written especially for the occasion, consisting of four movements by four of Hong Kong's leading composers. The rest of the programme was Saint-Saëns's Piano Concerto no. 2 (soloist: Max Sung), and Mussorgsky's *Night on Bald Mountain*. The East–West mix perfectly reflects a distinctive Hong Kong culture.

These festivals were organised following the riot in 1967. In 2003, Hong Kong was hard hit by SARS; Harbour Fest, a star-studded event, was subsequently held to lift the territory's spirit. HK Phil shared the stage with one of the 'Three Tenors' – José Carreras – and the Welsh singer Charlotte Church, whose celestial voice has captivated millions.

Princess Diana in the Audience

The orchestra was present at other official occasions too. On 8 November 1989, the Prince and Princess of Wales were in attendance at an all-British programme performed by the HK Phil at the Cultural Centre. The orchestra also played to mark Hong Kong's handover, taking part in the recording of Tan Dun's *Heaven Earth Mankind (Symphony 1997)* (the live premiere of the piece was given by the Asian Youth Orchestra). On top of that, HK Phil was featured at Tamar in a heavy downpour. During important anniversaries of the Handover, the orchestra has also played a part. For instance, HK Phil shared the stage with the Hong Kong Chinese Orchestra at the Hong Kong Coliseum during the celebration of HKSAR's twenty-fifth anniversary.

From Grantham to Lee

HK Phil belongs to Hong Kong. This is reflected in their honourable patrons. Hong Kong Governor Sir Alexander Grantham became SBO's honourable patron in 1949. HK Phil was inaugurated in 1957, basically taking over SBO's operation. Subsequent governors continued to be honourable patrons of HK Phil. Since the handover, the HKSAR's chief executive has been the orchestra's honourable patron. Flip through the orchestra's programme today, and one will see the name of Mr John Lee.

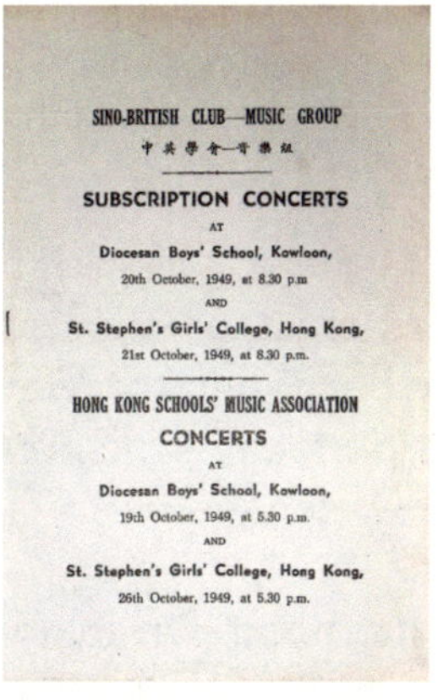

SINO-BRITISH CLUB—MUSIC GROUP

中英學會—音樂組

SUBSCRIPTION CONCERTS

AT

Diocesan Boys' School, Kowloon,

20th October, 1949, at 8.30 p.m

AND

St. Stephen's Girls' College, Hong Kong,

21st October, 1949, at 8.30 p.m.

HONG KONG SCHOOLS' MUSIC ASSOCIATION

CONCERTS

AT

Diocesan Boys' School, Kowloon,

19th October, 1949, at 5.30 p.m.

AND

St. Stephen's Girls' College, Hong Kong,

26th October, 1949, at 5.30 p.m.

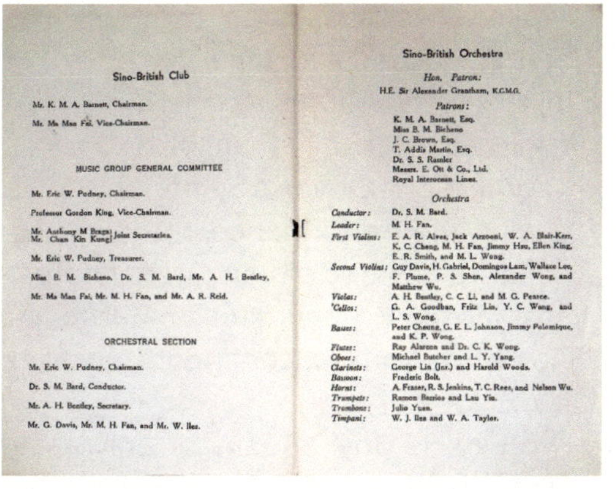

Sino-British Club

Mr. K. M. A. Barnett, Chairman.

Mr. Ma Man Fai, Vice-Chairman.

MUSIC GROUP GENERAL COMMITTEE

Mr. Eric W. Pudney, Chairman.

Professor Gordon King, Vice-Chairman.

Mr. Anthony M Braga / Mr. Chan Kin Kung } Joint Secretaries.

Mr. Eric W. Pudney, Treasurer.

Miss B. M. Bicheno, Dr. S. M. Bard, Mr. A. H. Bentley,

Mr. Ma Man Fai, Mr. M. H. Fan, and Mr. A. R. Reid.

ORCHESTRAL SECTION

Mr. Eric W. Pudney, Chairman.

Dr. S. M. Bard, Conductor.

Mr. A. H. Bentley, Secretary.

Mr. G. Davis, Mr. M. H. Fan, and Mr. W. Iles.

Sino-British Orchestra

Hon. Patron:

H.E. Sir Alexander Grantham, K.C.M.G.

Patrons:

K. M. A. Barnett, Esq.
Miss B. M. Bicheno
J. C. Brown, Esq.
T. Addis Martin, Esq.
Dr. S. S. Ramler
Messrs. E. Ott & Co., Ltd.
Royal Interocean Lines.

Orchestra

Conductor: Dr. S. M. Bard.
Leader: M. H. Fan.
First Violins: E. A. R. Alves, Jack Arzooni, W. A. Blair-Kerr, K. C. Cheng, M. H. Fan, Jimmy Hsu, Ellen King, E. R. Smith, and M. L. Wong.
Second Violins: Guy Davis, H. Gabriel, Domingos Lam, Wallace Lee, F. Plume, P. S. Shen, Alexander Wong, and Matthew Wu.
Violas: A. H. Bentley, C. C. Li, and M. G. Pearce.
'Cellos: G. A. Goodban, Fritz Lin, Y. C. Wang, and L. S. Wong.
Basses: Peter Cheung, G. E. L. Johnson, Jimmy Polomique, and K. P. Wong.
Flutes: Ray Alarcon and Dr. C. K. Wong.
Oboes: Michael Butcher and L. Y. Yang.
Clarinets: George Lin (Jnr.) and Harold Woods.
Bassoon: Frederic Bolt.
Horns: A. Fraser, R. S. Jenkins, T. C. Rees, and Nelson Wu.
Trumpets: Ramon Barrios and Lau Yin.
Trombone: Julio Yuen.
Timpani: W. J. Iles and W. A. Taylor.

Photo 20.1 and Photo 20.2: Sir Alexander Grantham's name appears on this SBO programme dated 1949.

2. It Represents Hong Kong

Photo 20.3: In 1988, Martin Poon (first left in the first row) represented Hong Kong on behalf of HK Phil as a member of the World Philharmonic Orchestra in Montreal. Courtesy of Martin Poon.

This photo is a perfect example of how HK Phil has represented Hong Kong. In 1988, the World Philharmonic Orchestra recruited, from all around the world, 106 orchestral players to gather in Montreal. HK Phil was one of the organisations invited. Violinist Martin Poon was sent to Canada to take part in this international concert, conducted by Françoise Legrand. Beethoven's Symphony no. 9, 'Ode to Joy', was performed. During the performance, three big screens on stage showed satellite-transmitted singing from choruses in San Francisco, Geneva, and Moscow. According to Martin, it was perfectly synchronised. Audience from six continents were able to watch the performance live.

'Ode to Joy' speaks of universal brotherhood. On that occasion, Martin, HK Phil, and Hong Kong joined the world to realise that vision.

Other players have represented Hong Kong in concerts of a similar nature. From 1999 to 2009, First Associate Concertmaster Leung Kin-fung spent time in Tokyo as part of the Super World Orchestra, which brought together concertmasters and principals from the world's leading orchestras. Conductors with whom he has worked in this global orchestra included Zubin Mehta, Bernard Haitink and Lorin Maazel.

Many of the orchestra's overseas tours were organised in association with the HKSAR government's Economic and Trade Offices, with HK Phil representing Hong Kong outside of its home. For instance, in November 2019, a huge event – Hong Kong Week – was mounted in Shanghai. HK Phil made an appearance in a concert along with local pianist Rachel Cheung, directed by Jaap van Zweden. A month before that, members of the orchestra were in London to receive the 2019 Orchestra of the Year Award at the ceremony organised by *Gramophone*. This was the result of the orchestra's recording of Wagner's *Ring* cycle. The award does not have a geographical implication, but this four-year performance-cum-recording project was sponsored by the HKSAR government; Naxos, which produced the CDs, is a company founded and deeply rooted in Hong Kong. It is therefore appropriate to see HK Phil as a Hong Kong representative in garnering the prestigious award.

3. It Is Engaged in Hong Kong

HK Phil actively takes part in Hong Kong's livelihood and promotes the arts in the territory. It synchronises with the pace of Hong Kong people, and in this way it is, in its essence, the 'Hong Kong' Philharmonic Orchestra.

Christmas, New Year, Easter

One way to engage in Hong Kong's livelihood is to organise special performances on special days. The orchestra has presented numerous Christmas, New Year and National Day concerts. Symphony of Christmas Angels, staged on 23 and 24 December 2011, is a classic example. The angelic voices came from another 'Hong Kong' organisation: the Hong Kong Children's Choir.

Photo 20.4: The Symphony of Christmas Angels concert in 2011.

New Year is celebrated in the Viennese musical tradition at HK Phil. For years, the orchestra has presented waltzes and polkas as local audiences eagerly look forward to the new year. In 2021, HK Phil teamed up with the Hong Kong Tourism Board in a joyful countdown with a big crowd at West Kowloon Cultural District.

Easter is also a major festival in Hong Kong. In 2013, with the reactivated HK Phil Chorus, the orchestra presented Handel's *Messiah*. The classic oratorio is apt for Christmas performances too. From 19 to 21 December 1980, Swiss-Chinese conductor Chen Liang-Sheng (first husband of pianist Martha Argerich) directed the HK Phil Choir and the orchestra in the same piece at the newly opened Queen Elizabeth Stadium. The British Council, the concert's sponsor, arranged for four leading British singers – Teresa Cahill (soprano), Claire Livingstone (mezzo-soprano), Keith Lewis (tenor), and Ian Caddy (bass) – to come to Hong Kong and take up the solo parts. For Christmas 2024, the orchestra presented the same work in the Mozart-edited, German-language version. This was HK Phil's first ever performance of this special version!

Bursting a Huge Balloon on Stage

The orchestra was assigned a major duty to help test the acoustics of the Cultural Centre. A few months before our cultural landmark was unveiled, the place was still a construction site. An informal concert took place at its concert hall. I was lucky enough to be part of the first audience in the hall. While HK Phil was playing, audio data was collected at different spots. Before the concert, a lady holding a huge balloon walked to centre stage. She then 'elegantly' burst the balloon with a needle. That loud noise was to test the hall's acoustics. Those who were present may remember that intriguing scene.

When the centre officially opened, HK Phil took part in the International Celebration of the Arts – a once-in-a-lifetime festival. Star performers including sopranos Joan Sutherland and Jessye Norman, conductor Richard Bonynge, and guitarist John Williams were stage partners with the orchestra.

Photo 20.5 (left): Poster of Hong Kong Cultural Centre's opening festival. Courtesy of LCSD.
Photo 20.6 (right): Guitarist John Williams. The conductor was Kenneth Schermerhorn. Courtesy of LCSD.

More New Venues

Whenever a sizeable concert venue opens in Hong – such as the Academic Community Hall and Tsuen Wan, Sha Tin and Tuen Mun Town Halls – it won't be long before HK Phil performs there. In this way the orchestra builds new audiences and at the same time fulfils its commitment to the community. On 26 February 1980, Yitkin Seow played Mendelssohn's Piano Concerto no. 1 in a concert as part of the Tsuen Wan Arts Festival. On 6 September 1985, the orchestra was featured in Tai Po Civic Centre's Inauguration Concert. In the same year on 4 March, the orchestra performed at Lut Sau Hall, taking part in the 5th Yuen Long Arts Festival.

Hong Kong Arts Festival

HK Phil made its Hong Kong Arts Festival debut in 1974 (the first festival was held in 1973, just before HK Phil turned professional) in a concert that included the *Butterfly Lovers' Concerto (by He Zhanhao and* Chen Gang) with the orchestra's music director Lim Kek-tjiang as soloist. In the following half-century, HK Phil has been a frequent participant in the festival. On top of concerts, the orchestra also accompanies the festival's operas and ballets.

Looking back, as early as 1955, SBO was an active player at the first Hong Kong Festival of Arts (which bears no relation to the present-day Hong Kong Arts Festival). On 5 April, the orchestra performed at the Empire Theatre in North Point as part of the festival. At the third festival in 1957, HK Phil had just taken over from SBO. A concert held on 31 October at HKU's Loke Yew was conducted by Arrigo Foa. The programme included Beethoven's Piano Concerto no. 3 (soloist: Geoffrey Tankard), and 'Spring' and 'Summer' from Joseph Haydn's *The Seasons*, with the chorus of the Hong Kong Oratorio Society.

HK Phil has contributed vastly to the development of the arts in Hong Kong, showcasing local performers including instrumentalists and singers; and among new works first performed by the orchestra, many have been written by local composers.

Tsang Fook, Cathay Pacific, and St. James Settlement

On 17 November 1966, the pre-professional HK Phil gave a concert at City Hall to mark the fiftieth anniversary of Tsang Fook Piano Company, which had been in operation before World War I. In 2006, it was the sixtieth anniversary of another time-honoured brand: Cathay Pacific. A birthday concert conducted by Edo de Waart was held at Cathay City. On 16 August 1968, HK Phil took part in a fundraising concert with proceeds going to St. James Settlement. The programme included Henryk Wieniawski's Violin Concerto no. 2, and the soloist was Y. S. Liu (who, forty years later, was elected chairman of HK Phil's Board of Governors).

Photo 20.7: Tsang Fook Piano Company Golden Jubilee Concert House Programme.

Hongkongers have many collective memories of these organisations; in fact, HK Phil is itself part of many collective memories too.

Different happenings trigger different sentiments in the community. In days of festivity, the orchestra brings the joy of music.

When it came to the 2020 COVID pandemic, the orchestra faced adversities like everyone else. One of HK Phil's responses was to mobilise its members and friends to come up with a virtual performance of 獅子山下 ('Below the Lion Rock'). Find out more in Chapter 34, 'When the Sky Isn't Blue'.

Cantopop

How 'Hong Kong' is the Phil? One may find an answer in Cantopop: an essential part of Hong Kong culture. From the Michael Kwan concerts in 1982 to HK Phil 50 – Symphonic Reunion in 2024, many Cantopop singers have collaborated with HK Phil. The number of concerts held, and the volume of audiovisual products generated, is enormous.

The chart in Chapter 39, 'Pop Goes the Phil', lists all the Cantopop concerts in which HK Phil has taken part. It may give us a further hint as to how 'Hong Kong' the Phil has been!

21 *Miss Hong Kong*

Was there ever a Miss Hong Kong winner who worked at the Phil?

Yes. Ethel Lau was crowned second runner-up in the first Miss Hong Kong Pageant organised by TVB (Television Broadcasts Limited) in 1973. She represented Hong Kong at the Pageant Miss Asia Quest 1974 in the Philippines and won three prizes. She was first runner-up, voted as 'Miss Friendship', and garnered the 'Miss Talent Prize' with her rendition of *Killing Me Softly with His Song*.

Ethel has a passion for classical music. Unlike fellow winners of the 1973 Miss Hong Kong Pageant—namely, Elaine Sun (champion) or Angie Chiu (fourth prize)—she chose a career in classical music over the entertainment business. After working briefly at TVB, she became HK Phil's Public Relations Officer in December 1975. She later became the orchestra's concert manager and marketing and promotions manager. She remembers that in the early days, the office only had five full-timers. Ethel was multi-tasking: she had to issue press releases, serve as emcee in concerts, produce house programmes, liaise with different parties, and get involved with translations. She was grateful that it was a cosy working team – everyone was eager to help out! After six years of service at the orchestra, she moved to Australia. To leave a workplace where she loved was not easy. It took her some time to get over that feeling of loss.

In 1976, while working at HK Phil, she sang (on her private capacity) in Bedřich Smetana's opera *The Bartered Bride*. Accompaniment was provided by the organisation she was serving – HK Phil.

Photo 21.1: The Czech opera *The Bartered Bride* was sung in Mandarin in 1976. It was presented by the Urban Council in association with HK Phil. The conductor was Wong Wing-hee. In addition to being a member of the chorus which was founded by her teacher Lin Siang-yuen, Ethel Lau also sang a small role in it. Courtesy of Ethel Lau.

Photo 21.2: Ethel Lau (middle) with colleagues Vennie Ho (left) and Silvana Li (right) at the HK Phil office. Courtesy of Ethel Lau.

Ethel's love of music was cultivated since childhood. She has three Grade 8 certificates in music theory, piano, and singing respectively! She was also a multitalented Miss Hong Kong who can sing art songs and opera arias!

22 *The Flagship Orchestra at the Flagship Theme Park*

Two flagships set sail together!

On 3 and 4 December 2021, in front of the Castle of Magical Dreams, Hong Kong Disneyland presented A Magical Nighttime Symphony with the HK Phil, bringing the blessings of Christmas to visitors. Under the direction of Chiu Tsang-hei, *Joy to the World* and *Jingle Bells* were played. The orchestra also played popular Disney songs such as *A Whole New World* and *Frozen Heart*. The medley *Prince and Princess* reminded everyone of many Disney protagonists. The audience was also treated to Dukas's *The Sorcerer's Apprentice* – an unforgettable moment in the movie *Fantasia*. The concert must have had a special appeal to a few adorable audience members too; in attendance were Mickey, Minnie, Donald, Daisy, Goofy, Anna and Elsa!

HK Phil's presence at Hong Kong Disneyland undoubtedly added an extra Hong Kong flavour to the theme park.

Photo 22.1: A Magical Nighttime Symphony, 2021.

23 *Wunderkinder*

The following musicians all have at least two things in common. First, they received training in Hong Kong and became highly accomplished musicians. Second, they have all performed with HK Phil.

- Yip Wing-sie was winner of the first prize and 'Lyre d'Or' at the 35th Concours International de Jeunes Chefs d'Orchestre de Besançon, France. At present, she is Hong Kong Sinfonietta's music director emeritus.
- Thomas Stumpf was winner of the Bösendorfer Prize. At the 1973 Edinburgh Festival, he was accompanist for soprano Edith Mathis's recital.
- Elim Chan, an internationally sought-after conductor, directed the First Night of the Proms in 2024 and the Last Night of the Proms in 2025. She was the first female winner of the Donatella Flick LSO Conducting Competition.
- Pianist David Oei appeared in Leonard Bernstein's Young People's Concert in 1966. He has recorded for nine recording labels.
- Lio Kuokman is Macao Orchestra's music director and principal conductor, and programme director of the Macao International Music Festival. He has conducted the Philadelphia Orchestra and Vienna Symphony Orchestra.
- Colleen Lee won the sixth prize at the International Chopin Piano Competition. Her discography includes an all-Chopin album released by the Fryderyk Chopin Institute.
- Perry So is the music director of the New Haven Symphony Orchestra. He has conducted the Los Angeles Philharmonic.
- Aristo Sham won both the Gold Medal and the Audience Prize at the Seventeenth Van Cliburn International Piano Competition in 2025. His winner's package includes three

years of individualised career management, along with concert tours in the United States and internationally.

Yesterday's Stars of Tomorrow

Thomas Stumpf was born in Shanghai in 1950. The family moved to Hong Kong and he subsequently studied at King George V School. After finishing his studies at the Mozarteum in Austria, he became a versatile musician. His biography begins like this: 'At age 16, he performed a Mozart concerto with the Hong Kong Philharmonic.'[1]

David Oei was also born in 1950. As a child, he studied piano under Tu Yueh-sien and garnered many prizes at the Hong Kong Schools Music Festival. Later, he moved to the United States. At present, he runs his own chamber music concert series in New York. Like Stumpf, he also begins his biography by quoting his first collaboration with HK Phil. He was only nine years old then.

Clearly, to be able to work with HK Phil at an early age is a remarkable experience.

Thomas Stumpf and David Oei worked with the pre-professional HK Phil. In fact, in the SBO years, precious opportunities such as these also fell to other promising young talents.

Playing a Concerto at Empire Theatre

On 10 June 1954, Irene Yuen teamed up with SBO to play César Franck's *Symphonic Variations*. A few months later, Mimi Chow was soloist in Beethoven's Piano Concerto no. 1. Not long after appearing at those concerts at Empire Theatre, they went abroad to pursue further studies. The two young musicians must have benefited much from their SBO experiences.

1 Thomas's brother Martin was a gifted pianist too. On 4 December 1963, at the age of 17, he played Mendelssohn's Piano Concerto no. 1 with HK Phil.

More budding musicians were featured at Empire Theatre. On 5 April 1955, it was the turn of the 16-year-old Hu Kwong. His father is the famous vocalist Jan Hu. He played Harold Perry's Concertino for Violin and Orchestra. On 5 July, Chiu Yee-ha played Mozart's Piano Concerto no. 23. Seven years later, she returned to Hong Kong to play with the London Philharmonic Orchestra (conductor: Malcolm Sargent) at City Hall to mark the opening of the new venue. She returned to play with the HK Phil on other occasions in both the orchestra's pre-professional and professional days.

Photo 23.1: Pianist Chiu Yee-ha.

Nancy Loo

Pianist Nancy Loo has a very close working relationship with HK Phil. Her piano teacher, Betty Drown, was one of the founders of the Sino-British Club and a keen advocate of SBO. Along with her husband, Drown saw the need for Hong Kong to have one more professional grand piano. Eventually, they bought one, which was used at public concerts. Upon her return to the United Kingdom, Betty gave that instrument as a gift to Nancy – one of her favourite students.

In the early 1960s, Nancy made her debut with the orchestra in Schumann's

Photo 23.2: Nancy Loo performed Saint-Saëns's Piano Concerto no. 2 with HK Phil, conducted by Hans Günter Mommer, in 1979.

concerto under Arrigo Foa. She recalls that the maestro looked rather serious! More collaborations followed, including an outdoor performance of the *Youth Piano Concerto* at Kowloon Park. The conductor this time was Lim Kek-tjiang. Her collaboration with Hans Günther Mommer was in Saint-Saëns's Piano Concerto no. 2. She also played along with Gabriel Kwok in the same composer's *Carnival of the Animals* under the baton of Kenneth Schermerhorn. Under the direction of Yip Wing-sie, Nancy and Gabriel were filmed in the same piece, which was made into an educational video of the same title. Nancy is grateful to the orchestra for the nourishment: she was featured as soloist with HK Phil in Liszt's Piano Concerto no. 1, the same piece she subsequently played at the Marguerite Long International Piano Competition (now The Long-Thibaud International Competition); in which she was a winner too. Looking back, Nancy reminiscences about the sweet excitement then: 'Whenever I got a chance to play with the orchestra, it meant I could return to my lovely hometown – Hong Kong.'

Blossom with Music

HK Phil has done much in cultivating local talents. Colleen Lee has this to say: 'The orchestra is one of my major mentors. In 2006, shortly after I became a winner at the International Chopin Piano Competition, along with Tom Lee Music, HK Phil offered me a performance platform to give a recital.'

It is important to provide a platform for young musicians. To be able to perform in a professional manner is vital to their artistic development. Violinist Ivan Chan started working with the

Photo 23.3: An advertisement for Colleen Lee's recital in a HK Phil house programme.

orchestra when he was thirteen. Later, he studied in the United States. He now teaches at The Hong Kong Academy for Performing Arts (HKAPA). He is a chamber music specialist.

In September 2007, Edo de Waart's delightful idea came true: he conducted all five of Beethoven's piano concertos, each featuring a young soloist. The first, second, and third concertos were played by Aristo Sham (11), Vanessa Wong (14), and Rachel Cheung (15).

Photo 23.4: Poster for Swire New Generation Series: Beethoven + 5 Pianists.

In recent years, more young violinists have worked with the orchestra. Paloma So was 9 and Hannah Tam was 12 when they first played a Mozart concerto with HK Phil. In 2017, the 12-year-old Paloma was on the stage of Swire Symphony Under the Stars, playing Franz Waxman's *Carmen Fantasy* in front of a huge crowd. At the same occasion, the 14-year-old Johnson Li played Chopin's *Grande Polonaise Brillante*.

Photo 23.5 and Photo 23.6: Edo de Waart with Aristo Sham (left) and Vanessa Wong (right) while rehearsing for Swire New Generation Series: Beethoven + 5 Pianists concerts.

Photo 23.7 and Photo 23.8: Paloma So (left) and Johnson Li (right) at Swire Symphony Under the Stars in 2017.

Paloma So and David Oei were both nine when they made their HK Phil debuts. Warren Lee, however, may have been the youngest soloist ever to share the stage with the orchestra in a large-scale concert.

Tiny Hands in a Gigantic Stadium

The six-year-old Warren Lee's televised performance with the orchestra, of Handel's *The Arrival of the Queen of Sheba* at Hong Kong Coliseum, earned him the title of 'prodigy'. Warren recalls that it was a precious opportunity for him to learn. Many more performance invitations subsequently came. He could have built a career without even entering a competition. Warren is thankful to his teacher, who, at the time, turned down many performance and interview opportunities to ensure that Warren's talent developed in the right environment, and at the right pace. The grown-up Warren has continued to be 'nourished' by HK Phil. He has said with a smile, 'I collaborated with the orchestra as a concerto player when I was in my 20s, 30s, and now – 40s.' Aside from playing concertos, he often teams up with members of the orchestra in chamber performances. Playing Messiaen's *Quatuor pour la fin*

Photo 23.9: Warren Lee made his HK Phil debut at the age of six. Courtesy of Warren Lee.

du temps ('Quartet for the End of Time') was what he found most memorable.

In addition to fostering young soloists, HK Phil has established a lasting partnership with HKAPA, allowing its budding musicians to play along with the orchestra's players and get inspired. One student who benefited from the programme in 2009 recalls:

> Perry So directed us [HKAPA Symphony Orchestra] in Stravinsky's *Firebird* suite, and Wagner's Prelude from *Tristan und Isolde*. That was absolutely unforgettable. To a great extent, it also paved the way for me to become an orchestral player. After serving as concertmaster in some orchestras, I was further stimulated to be a conductor. I saw connections in all these. Playing along with HK Phil has unquestionably changed my life.
>
> – Mark Hui (Principal Conductor, Hong Kong Festival Orchestra)

From 2021 to 2024, the Orchestra Academy Hong Kong programme was implemented. It was the first programme to be jointly directed by the orchestra and HKAPA's School of Music. The programme was funded by TrustTomorrow of the Swire Group Charitable Trust. Its purpose was to provide professional training for HKAPA's graduates, facilitating development in their careers as orchestral players. HK Phil's chief executive Benedikt Fohr said, 'In an audition, our first concern is the artistic standard. This programme provides young players with more practical experience, so that they may be more prepared for future auditions.'

Even for local players who did not go on to audition for HK Phil, the programme helped to increase their competitiveness in the international orchestral scene.

Bernard van Zuiden Music Fund

Established in 1983, the Bernard van Zuiden Music Fund has a mandate to nurture local musicians. Mr van Zuiden was a Dutch businessman who lived in Hong Kong for years. Before his passing, he wished to set up a trust fund. He approached the orchestra, which became a trustee. Applications are open to young Chinese talent from Hong Kong. Successful candidates receive financial aid for overseas music training. In the past four decades, scholarship recipients included Giulietta Tam (organ), Colleen Lee (piano), HK Phil's Percussionist Sophia Woo, Associate Principal Cor Anglais Kwan Sheung-fung, Co-Principal Bassoon Toby Chan, and former Principal Second Violin Fan Ting.

On the feeling of being a scholarship recipient, Colleen Lee shares: 'I want to thank the Bernard van Zuiden Music Fund, and HK Phil as a trustee. They did not just provide the scholarship for me to further my studies overseas, it was also an assertion – an encouragement to me as I pursue my artistic development.'

Other accomplished young local musicians have associated with the orchestra as freelancers. This is the case especially when it comes to extra-large works, or if an instrument not commonly heard in an orchestra (such as the organ or saxophone) is called for. It is a win-win scenario: while making a contribution to the orchestra, the players also gain practical orchestral experience.

Gifted Baton-Wavers

To nurture a good conductor requires time and space. Isolated performances may not achieve much. HK Phil created the resident conductor position in 1984. The first successful candidate was the young John Lau, who was born and raised in Hong Kong. He was succeeded by Yip Wing-sie, Choi Ho-man, Harmen Cnossen, and Lio Kuokman. Some others have served as assistant conductors: Perry So (later promoted to associate conductor), Vivian Ip, and Gerard Salonga.

The longest-serving resident conductor was Yip Wing-sie. Apart from conducting subscription concerts, promotional concerts, school concerts, community concerts, and pop concerts, she also had to attend rehearsals, offer assistance to conductors, take sectional rehearsals, train the HK Phil Chorus, and serve as emcee. Once, she stood in for Music Director David Atherton, who fell sick. She has expressed gratitude to have received such all-round training. To her, it was treasurable experience.

Finally, a word about Lio Kuokman.

Photo 23.10: John Lau, HK Phil's first resident conductor.

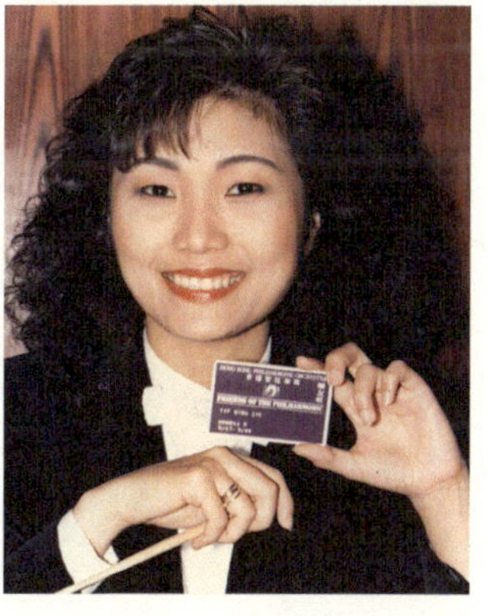

Photo 23.11: Yip Wing-sie with her Friends of the Philharmonic membership card. She was engaged in a lot of the orchestra's promotional activities.

Happy Birthday to Me . . .

Lio Kuokman is a busy bee, always flying here and there to conduct different orchestras. He says of HK Phil:

> I was a secondary school student when I first listened to them. The orchestra came to Macao and gave a concert at Cathedral of the Nativity of Our Lady. *The Firebird* was in the programme. The sonic effect was so memorable! When I first played with the orchestra as soloist, I teamed up with my brother Kuok-Wai in Saint-Saëns's *The Carnival of the Animals*. Later, I decided to become a conductor. HK Phil gave me a lot of opportunities to direct different performances. Over the years, players have witnessed my growth and transformation. We have cultivated close ties. Four years ago, I was originally to quarantine for fourteen days before directing a performance. Suddenly, the pandemic escalated, and the quarantine period was extended to twenty-one days. Unexpectedly, I was alone in my hotel room on my fortieth birthday. Some colleagues, however, prepared a big surprise for me. They sent a birthday cake! Then, from a distance, they waved to the birthday boy, who was standing beside the windowpane.

Kuokman ate that birthday cake all by himself – yet he did not feel lonely. That heartwarming friendship accompanied him.

24 *Music Therapy for Rachel*

During COVID, many soloists were unable to come to Hong Kong as planned. Pianist Rachel Cheung substituted some of them, and turned out having more opportunities to play with HK Phil. Back in 2003, she appeared with the orchestra as soloist in Mozart Whiz Kids. She was 12 then (the other prodigy was the 14-year-old Lio Kuok-Wai). More collaborations followed, but she found this one particularly special: in a series of school concerts, she played the finale of Beethoven's Piano Concerto no. 3 about ten times! In 2019, she was in Guangzhou, playing while directing Beethoven's Piano Concerto no. 4. She is indebted to Concertmaster Jing Wang for helping her to communicate effectively with the orchestra. Everything went well!

Another collaboration with the HK Phil was full of drama. Rachel told me the story:

> While in Moscow in 2005, I suffered from meningitis and was hospitalised. For quite some time, my condition was serious. Right at that moment, however, my dad who was with me, received a call from my teacher Ms Elenor Wong. She asked him to tell me that HK Phil planned to invite me to take part in a complete Beethoven piano concerto series! This was like a cardiac stimulant. I told myself 'I must recover!' With that determination, my health improved quickly. Having stayed at the hospital for one month, I finally made my way home. On the return journey, I was accompanied by medical staff who came all the way from Hong Kong to look after me. That was so touching.

Photo 24.1: On 25 September 2023, Rachel Cheung performed with HK Phil's Woodwind Quintet at A Musical Paintbox concert as part of the West Kowloon Cultural District's Tea House Chamber Music Series.

25 *Tunefully Ever After*

HK Phil made the world's first recording of Mahler's Symphony no. 10 (excerpts Ed. W. Mengelberg and C. Dopper for Concert Orchestra) and added to the world one more box set of Wagner's *Ring* cycle.

From its first *Butterfly Lovers Concerto* LP in 1978 to *The Ring: An Orchestral Adventure* in 2025, HK Phil has made numerous recordings. Some can be heard online too. The orchestra's discography tells the story of the unique path it has taken.

Photo 25.1: HK Phil's first recording (released by Polydor) included the *Butterfly Lovers' Concerto* with Lim Kek-han on the violin. The conductor was the orchestra's second Music Director Hans Günter Mommer.

To Record a Romantic Story

The *Butterfly Lovers* was an obvious choice for the orchestra's premiere recording in 1978. Obviously, the predominantly Chinese population of Hong Kong was a consideration. On side one of the recording, there are a few delightful Chinese pieces including Li Huanzhi's *Spring Festival Overture*, He Luting's *Night Party*, Mao Yuan and Liu Tieshan's *Dance of the Yao People*, and Wu Zuqiang and Du Mingxin's *Three Dances from the Ballet – The Mermaid*. Sales of the recording were not bad. The 1982 release of the album *Colourful Clouds*, however, was a sweeping success. Between *Butterfly Lovers* and *Colourful Clouds*, HK Phil took part in another recording: it was under the direction of

Ling Tung in a collaboration with soprano Barbara Fei in Doming Lam's *Three Night Songs of Li-Po.*

Platinum

Colourful Cloud brought a refreshing feel to music lovers. It again featured Chinese works, including folk songs such as *The Embroidered Purse* and art songs such as *How Can I Forget Him* by Zhao Yuanren. Featuring recently developed digital recording technologies, the promising conductor Kenneth Jean (who was not yet thirty), and effective publicity, the album quickly achieved gold and then platinum awards!

Photo 25.2: Open-reel tapes of *Colourful Cloud.*

Empress Wu, Qiu Jin, and Concubine Yang

Riding on this success, HK Phil issued more albums with similar repertoires. Along with more folk songs such as *Under the Silver Moon* and *Flower Drum Song*, they recorded theme music from movies and soap operas such as 不了情 ('Everlasting Love') and 上海灘 ('The Bund of Shanghai'), and vintage popular Shanghai songs such as 夜上海 ('Shanghai Nights') and 如果沒有你 ('If I Don't Have You'). There was an album with the catchy title of *12 Heroines of Imperial China*, which put prominent historical female figures into the limelight.

In addition to these more popular tunes, HK Phil also issued recordings of Chinese symphonic works such as Ding Shande's *Long March Symphony*, Chen Gang's violin concerto 'Wang Zhaojun', Liu Zhu's zhonghu concerto 'Su Wu', and Chen Peixun's *Fantasia on Cantonese Folk Themes*. Contemporary composers including Toshiro Mayuzumi,

Bright Sheng, and Tan Dun – for example, *Heaven Earth Mankind (Symphony 1997)* – have HK Phil albums exclusively of their works. In 1986, HK Phil also made a recording of works by several modern composers to mark the first Hong Kong staging of International Music Day, organised by the International Society of Contemporary Composers (ISCM).

Regarding general Western classical music, HK Phil has recorded many 'rarities' including Wagner's little-known overtures and marches. Richard Strauss is famous for his operas and symphonic poems, but the orchestra was interested in his D minor Symphony. Jules Massenet is also noted for his operas, but HK Phil presented his orchestral suites.

César Cui, Ferruccio Busoni, and Alexander Glazunov are well-known composers. However, despite huge outputs, their works have seldom been recorded. These masters all have featured albums recorded by HK Phil. In fact, Glazunov has three!

Scarcity Breeds Value

There are numerous versions of recordings of standard repertoire in the market. Even great composers have little-known works that are rarely recorded, if at all. HK Phil helped to fill the gap.

David Atherton is a champion of contemporary music. After taking over the helm as Music Director in the 1990s, he recorded a few albums of Stravinsky's lesser-known music, such as *Quatre études pour orchestre* ('Four Etudes for Orchestra'), and the ballet *La baiser de la fée* ('The Fairy's Kiss'). Two seldom-heard symphonies by Kurt Weill were also recorded by HK Phil.

One of HK Phil's recent releases is a live performance of Tchaikovsky's Piano Concerto no. 1, and Symphony no. 5. The orchestra has not been too keen with recording main mainstream concert works like these. In the past, they have recorded Brahms's twenty-one

Hungarian Dances, Fauré's Requiem, and Shostakovich's Symphonies nos. 5 and 9. There is also an album featuring coloratura Beverly Hoch, and compilation of choral works sung by the Winchester College Chapel Choir, both with the orchestra in an accompanying role. These two recordings put a little music of the Baroque and Classical eras into HK Phil's discography.

Next, let us look at two stunning achievements: Wagner's *Ring* cycle, and Mahler's Symphony no. 10.

14-CD Set

Photo 25.3: The 14-CD set of Wagner's *Der Ring des Nibelungen*.

From 2015 to 2018, HK Phil presented one part of the *Ring* set per year. Naxos recorded the performances live and released a set of CDs each year. The result is a 14-CD set with a total of 14 hours and 55 minutes of music. HK Phil was named Orchestra of the

Photo 25.4: HK Phil and Music Director Jaap van Zweden. In 2019, the HK Phil won the Orchestra of the Year award from the prestigious British classical music magazine *Gramophone*, becoming the first orchestra in Asia to receive this honour.

Year at the 2019 Gramophone Classical Music Awards ceremony – regarded as the 'Oscars' of classical music – in London. This was an acknowledgement of the orchestra's contributions to classical music recording of the past year.

Looking back, there were quite a few hurdles to overcome to forge this *Ring*. First, huge funding was needed. The orchestra first applied for the Mega Arts and Cultural Events Fund, but the application was not successful. The HKSAR government subsequently sponsored the project through the Contestable Funding Scheme for the Major Performing Arts Groups.

Second, the work calls for quite a few highly accomplished singers, and not all voices are well suited to sing the *Ring*. HK Phil did not have enough time to engage the ideal singers years ahead. In the end, the recording featured three Brünnhildes and two Siegfrieds. Luckily there was just one Wotan: the famed Matthias Goerne. The role was new to him, and his involvement certainly drew more attention to this *Ring* cycle.

Third, as it was in a concert setting, singers had to stand in front of the orchestra on stage. When it came to very loud moments, players had to be careful not to overpower the singers, while sustaining the intensity.

Fourth, in a similar vein, the tempo, dynamics and articulations taken at two different performances may very well be different. This was challenging at the post-production stage. However, more rehearsal time (two extra weeks) was allocated for this grand project, which helped to solve the problem.

The *Ring* is genuinely a sensation. For Wagner aficionados and members of Wagner societies around the world, to be able to hear the *Ring* in Bayreuth is a pilgrimage. The orchestra successfully gave the HK debut of the tetralogy and went further to earn a prestigious award.

No wonder media organisations from many countries were eager to report the news.

Mahler Unveiled

Photo 25.5: HK Phil's album features Shostakovich's Symphony no. 10 and Mahler's Symphony no. 10.

HK Phil has many premiere recordings under its belt. This version of the Mahler Symphony no. 10, however, came with a special story.

Mahler passed away in 1911, leaving behind the unfinished Tenth Symphony. His conductor friend and loyal follower Willem Mengelberg laboured over the manuscripts and led the performance of the first and third movements in 1924. Nearly one century later, in December 2019, HK Phil played that version again, and a recording was subsequently released in 2022.

There are different versions of Mahler's Tenth. To be able to record one of them for the first time in history is quite something!

The latest HK Phil recording project is its first collaboration with Deutsche Grammophon. The album serves as a sequel to the *Ring* cycle – titled *The Ring: An Orchestral Adventure*, which is an arrangement of the work by Henk de Vlieger. Concertmaster Jing Wang remarks on the project, 'I notice that HK Phil's strings sound has changed. We have a signature sound now – that *Ring* cycle sound which is a bright and virtuosic sound. It is the right time to do it, we have the right sound for it.'

Alongside physical audio products, HK Phil has also reached music lovers through cyberspace. To mark the 200th anniversary of the birth of Bruckner, HK Phil performed the composer's Symphony no. 9 – for the first time – to open its 2024/25 season. This performance, directed by Tarmo Peltokoski, was made available on Deutsche Grammophon's online streaming platform Stage Plus (STAGE+).

Similar plans are underway with the orchestra signing a deal with Apple in cross promotion of the Orchestra's recording available on Apple Music and Apple Music Classical. An Apple Store event was presented in August 2024, featuring the adoption of Dolby Atmos and Apple's Spatial Audio technology in HK Phil classical music recordings to a broad audience.

At the beginning of this chapter, I mention that HK Phil's discography tells the story of the unique path which the orchestra has taken. Such uniqueness also lies in the orchestra's association with Cantopop. From Michael Kwan in 1982 to Hacken Lee in 2023, the number of audio and visual products generated is enormous (see Chapter 39, 'Pop Goes the Phil').

The following companies and labels have released audio and video recordings for HK Phil (not counting pop concerts):

- Decca
- Deutsche Grammophon
- GMN
- HK Records
- Hong Kong Philharmonic Orchestra
- IMP Classics
- Intimacy of Creativity
- Marco Polo
- MCA Classics
- Navona
- Naxos
- Philips
- SOMM Recordings
- SONY Classical
- Virgin Classics

26 *Backstage Masseurs*

One of the major challenges posed by the *Ring* cycle is its length. For instance, *Das Rheingold* runs for two hours and thirty-three minutes non-stop! Although *Götterdämmerung* is in different acts, the total duration is four hours and twenty-three minutes. Concertmaster Jing Wang is still in awe: '*Götterdämmerung* was the most exhausting experience of my life. There were so many notes. Utmost concentration was required for the performance. There were a lot of sectional rehearsals for the third act. The performances were recorded live. We had to concentrate all the time.' Double bass player Jonathan Van Dyke also remarks, 'At patching sessions, players had to stay alert and sit still for long hours, so as not to make a noise accidentally. The stress level is multiplied.'

All these factors contributed to muscle tension.

The orchestra was well prepared! During concerts, masseurs were on standby backstage. It wasn't just necks, shoulders, backs or waists that were treated – overall, it was a holistically beneficial experience!

27 *Evolution of the Ticket*

Let's begin by looking at how SBO and HK Phil's ticket prices compare to Hongkongers' livelihoods in past decades.

1955 – SBO played at Empire Theatre as part of the first Hong Kong Festival of Arts. Tickets were priced from HK$1 to HK$5. A copy of *Wah Kiu Yat Po* (a Chinese newspaper) was twenty cents then.

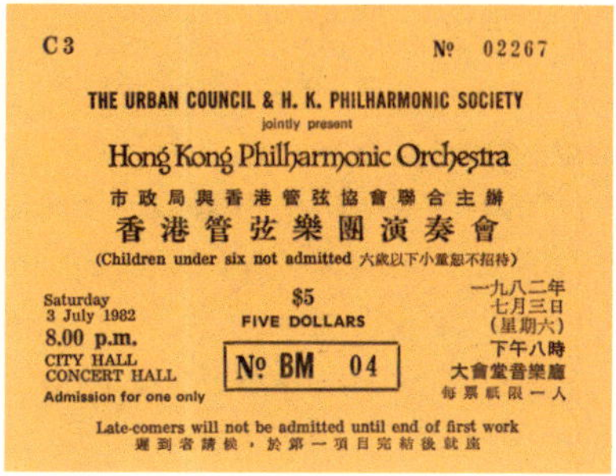

Photo 27.1: A ticket to the season-closing concert on 3 July 1982.

1965 – HK Phil was on hire to accompany pianist Priscilla King in a performance of concertos by Mozart and Mendelssohn. There was also a Haydn sonata in this concert presented by Bernard Ho. Tickets were priced from HK$3 to HK$5. A bowl of wonton noodles cost around thirty cents then.

1974 – HK Phil's first professional season: ticket prices for a subscription concert ranged from HK$4 to HK$10. When the first McDonalds restaurant opened in January 1975, a hamburger cost HK$1.6.

1984 – Normal ticket prices of a HK Phil concert at City Hall were HK$20 to HK$80. Tsuen Wan Town Hall concerts charged a little less, at HK$8 to HK$30. When star singers Leslie Cheung, Anita Mui, and David Lui appeared with the orchestra at the Hong Kong Coliseum (conductor: Michael Lai), ticket prices ranged from HK$20 to HK$90. Back then, a serving of pork chop rice at Fairwood fast food restaurant cost HK$8.5.

1994 – Tickets for the HK Phil concert featuring Ju Hee Suh performing Liszt's Piano Concerto no. 2 were HK$50 to HK$190. At the time, a copy of *ELLE* magazine cost HK$40.

What do you think about the figures above? As well as a nostalgic look back, the evolution of HK Phil's ticket prices is perhaps more revealing.

As for the 2024/25 concert season, many factors affect pricings: the nature of the concert, the soloist, the programme, production costs, and the number of seats with obstructed views.

Take a look at the top-price tickets, for example. A ticket for star tenor Jonas Kaufmann's Opera Gala was priced at HK$1,980. The season-opening concert with Tarmo Peltokoski conducting Bruckner's Ninth and Daniele Gatti conducting Mahler's Third were both HK$880. The season finale with Jaap van Zweden conducting Brahms's Fourth and Tan Dun's *Tea: A Mirror of Soul* were HK$680 and HK$520, respectively.

This is in line with recent trends vis-à-vis the pricings of other performing arts events. Financial arrangements, marketing strategies, flexibility with Urbtix (Hong Kong's ticketing system), and the audience's degree of acceptance are but a few of the factors that affect pricing of individual events. In the case of Joe Hisaishi's 2023 concerts, for example, ticket prices were set at HK$1,980, HK$1,480, and HK$680. On top of that, a real-name registration ticketing system was adopted, and music-lovers had to register and enter a draw. Despite all that, the oversubscription rate was still high.

Ticket Prices and Popularity

To certain extent, ticket prices reflect how popular an artist is. Diva pianist Yuja Wang, who has collaborated with HK Phil on a few occasions, is a good example. The following chart speaks for itself.

Table 27.1: Ticket prices for Yuja Wang's concerts with HK Phil

Year	Ticket price (HK$)
2010	$280, $200, $140, and $100
2015	$680, $480, $320, and $220
2017	$880, $680, $480, and $380

Perlman

Decades ago, ticket prices for a handful of concerts were fine-tuned. When Itzhak Perlman played with the HK Phil on 25 June 1975, he was already a sought-after violinist. Ticket prices went up a little, from the normal HK$2, HK$5, HK$10, and HK$15, to HK$10, HK$20, HK$30, HK$40, and HK$50. That was a three- to five-fold increase.

Other than upward adjusted prices, there have been special-offer ticket prices too.

One-Dollar Concerts

Some restaurants offer a crazily discounted dish (such as 'HK$1 whole chicken') to attract customers. In HK Phil's case, there were HK$1 concerts to build new audiences too! In 1965, the Urban Council started organising a series of popular concerts at City Hall. For a few years, tickets for these shows were all set at HK$1. Darwin Chen, City Hall's manager who devised the scheme, remarked, 'To watch a movie, front row seats cost HK$1; taxi meters started at HK$1 on Kowloon side, and HK$1.5 on Hong Kong side.'

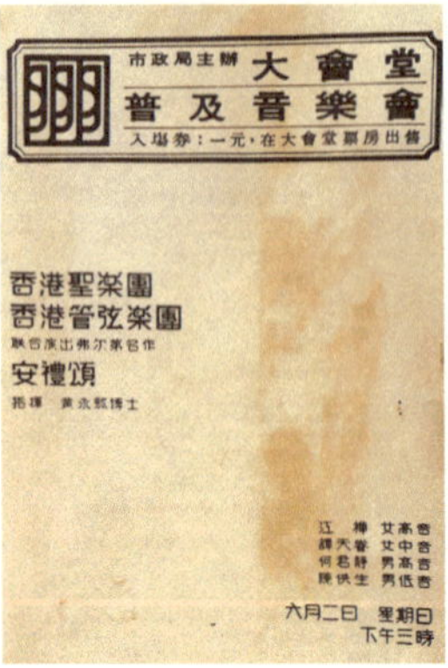

Photo 27.2: One of HK Phil's One-Dollar Concerts. Courtesy of Hong Kong Oratorio Society.

Cost of a Win-or-Place Bet

On 16 December 1979, HK Phil gave a family concert to a crowd of more than 10,000 at Sha Tin Racecourse. Tickets were priced at HK$5, which was incidentally the cost of a win-or-place bet at the Happy Valley horse races.

Birthday Offers

On 6 September 1985, HK Phil unveiled Tai Po Civic Centre with an opening concert. All tickets were sold at HK$10.

In 1992, the Hong Kong Arts Festival celebrated their twentieth birthday. Groups including HK Phil, Hong Kong Chinese Orchestra, and Hong Kong Dance Company were invited to take part in the Hong Kong Performing Arts Day. All shows were priced at HK$20.

Photo 27.3: Poster for the Tai Po Civic Centre Commissioning Concert.

The orchestra turned fifty in the 2023/24 season. To mark this momentous occasion, tickets for two selected concerts were all priced at HK$50. In some other concerts, a fixed number of tickets were sold at HK$50. Throughout the whole season, 5,000 such golden-jubilee tickets were offered to music-lovers.

This arrangement reminds one of Lea Salonga's concert at Sha Tin Town Hall in 2016. All tickets were sold at HK$50 and HK$100 only, making it possible for more people to watch the diva live. This was a wise move! At the concert, Lea Salonga sang some songs in Tagalog for the Filipino audience. It was a joyful occasion.

Even Lower Ticket Prices?

It should be free then! HK Phil has played for free in shopping malls and MTR stations. Musicians have also visited hospitals, elderly homes, and a prison to give free shows. During COVID, many performances were put online at no charge. HK Phil has a long tradition of giving free concerts. More than half a century ago, on 11 January 1974, HK Phil gave their first professional concert. The month before, as a professional group, the orchestra had already appeared on Rediffusion Television (RTV) on 1 December, and it gave another free public concert at Kowloon Park on 16 December.

Photo 27.4 and Photo 27.5: The pre-professional HK Phil appeared on RTV in the 1960s. Courtesy of Kathy Lam.

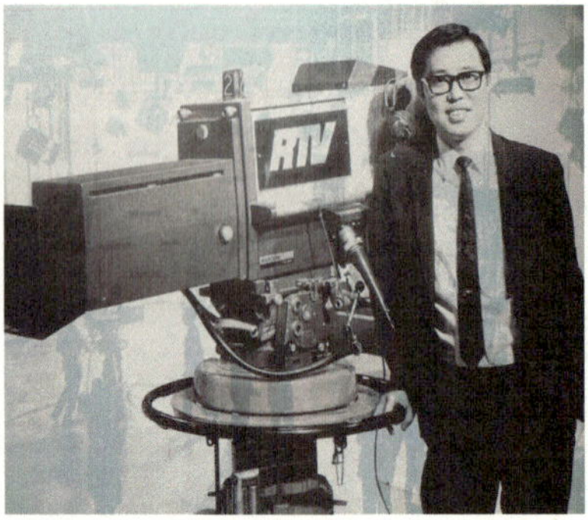

Photo 27.6: SBO former violinist and composer Doming Lam was RTV's producer. He was instrumental in showcasing the HK Phil on the TV station. Courtesy of Kathy Lam.

More Outreach

One of HK Phil's mandates is to promote music. Hence, the orchestra has always performed at schools and organised performances for students at concert venues.

Apart from the education sector, there have been a lot of promotional concerts. For example, on 22 December 1981, the orchestra gave a free Christmas concert at Lut Sau Hall, Yuen Long. From the 1990s, Symphony Under the Stars has become more and more popular as a free annual outdoor mega-event.

Photo 27.7: Due to COVID restrictions, the 2020 Swire Symphony Under the Stars was moved online. Under the direction of Lio Kuokman, the performance was filmed at Cultural Centre Concert Hall. It was more a Symphony Under the House Lights.

Other free community concerts included two shows on 24 and 25 October 2014. Vladimir Ashkenazy was seen conducting Rachmaninov's Symphony no. 2 and three works by Jean Sibelius at HKU. Sometimes, this kind of performance incorporates an educational element. On 25 and 26 February 2007, Edo de Waart directed the orchestra in Beethoven's Symphony no. 2 with an introduction by HK Phil's Chief Executive Michael MacLeod. The orchestra was reversed to face the small crowd who were seated near the organ. The orchestra and conductor were closer to the audience than usual. The sound was surprisingly good too.

On 13 June 2023, there was a Swire Classic Insights: Great Overtures concert. The conductor was the eminent André Orozco-Estrada. The performance standard was so high that some audience members jokingly asked, 'Was that concert also a music director audition?'

These free shows are great. Let's have more!

Photo 27.8: Swire Classic Insights: Great Overtures concert directed by Andrés Orozco-Estrada.

28 *Real-Name Tickets*

In 2022, when the sensational Hong Kong boy group MIRROR put on their shows at the Hong Kong Coliseum, real-name registration for ticket sales was adopted to prevent scalping. However, the first large-scale Hong Kong event to implement this system actually featured HK Phil.

In 2018, Joe Hisaishi collaborated with the orchestra for the second time. Tickets to the three concerts quickly sold out. Some people put tickets online for sale and asked for extremely high prices. This triggered a lot of grievances among music-lovers. The media covered the story widely, and it became a major PR challenge for the orchestra. To alleviate the situation, the orchestra entered into discussions with URBTIX and the Cultural Centre. Eventually, Hong Kong's first-ever real-name ticketing system was implemented for the additional show on 5 May.

Joe Hisaishi worked with HK Phil for the third time in June 2023. With five years' experience, the orchestra made similar arrangements, but applicable to all shows. How did the system work?

First, anyone who was interested in buying tickets had to register online. Each person had to provide an email address, telephone number, and credit card information, and could buy only one or two tickets. In the end, the orchestra received 45,000 applications. Of these, 13,000 were duplicates. Six thousand out of the 32,000 valid registrations successfully bought tickets. The success rate was about 19%. On show days, audience members had to be at the Cultural Centre foyer ninety minutes early. After checking the real-name ticket and proof of identity, staff members put wrist bands on audience members to allow their entry into the concert hall.

Photo 28.1: Joe Hisaishi real-name ticket booth.

HK Phil's Director of Marketing Dennis Wu said, 'We implemented and continued with the real-name system so that everyone may have a fair chance to enjoy the show. Having said that, although hurdles were set for the sale of tickets, we cannot rule out the possibility of someone trying to find loopholes in the system. Our intention was to increase the difficulty for scalping.'

On the topic of difficulties, I am reminded of that wrist band, which reads 'JOE HISAISHI IN CONCERT'. I wanted it as a keepsake, so I elected not to cut it. This turned out to be a challenge. I spent two minutes trying to take it off; and when I eventually succeeded, it left a thin bruise line on my wrist. At least I was able to take picture of it alongside the programme and my personalised ticket.

Photo 28.2: House programme, ticket and wristband for Joe Hisaishi's concerts in 2023. Photo credit: Jimmy Shiu.

29 *Subscriptions of Yesteryear*

Subscription models represent a major channel for the orchestra to sell tickets. A subscription was launched during the HK Phil's first professional season (1974/75). There were four series of performances: symphonic concerts, solo recitals, chamber orchestra concerts, and promenade concerts. Let us examine what marketing and programming strategies were adopted in the last millennium.

Table 29.1: HK Phil's first season subscription

Subscription series	Number of programmes	Number of performance(s) per programme	Prices for single tickets (HK$)	Subscription fee (HK$)	Average ticket price (HK$)	Top price discount
Symphonic concerts[1]	12	3	$4–$10	$40–$100	$3.30–$8.30	17%
Solo recitals[2]	12	1	$3–$8	$30–$80	$2.50–$6.70	17%
Chamber orchestra concerts[3]	10	1	$4–$9.50	$30–$80	$3–$8	16%
Promenade concerts[4]	10	2	$3–$6.50	$20–$50	$2–$5	23%

1 Symphonic concerts were held on Fridays (blue series), Saturdays (green series), and Sundays (red series). Large-scale symphonic works by composers such as Tchaikovsky, Brahms, Dvořák, and Shostakovich were played. Artists who concertised internationally were invited to be soloists.

2 Recitals by soloists who appeared at symphonic concerts were held on Tuesdays.

3 Chamber orchestra concerts happened on Saturdays and Sundays. Medium-sized orchestral works and Baroque pieces were played. Local musicians, HK Phil's principal players, and soloists from Asian countries were invited to play concertos.

4 Promenade concerts took place on Sundays at 3.00 p.m. (orange series) and 7.00 p.m. (purple series). Popular classics and film music were programmed.

Patron Subscribers

In addition to all the benefits enjoyed by regular subscribers, patron subscribers had more privileges. The costs for becoming a patron subscriber were HK$150 (chamber orchestra concerts), HK$250 (solo recitals), and HK$300 to HK$500 (symphonic concerts).

Discounts

Observant readers may notice that subscribers to the lowest price category of the Promenade series received an attractive 33% discount. The maximum discount rate for the 2024/25 subscription season was 30%.

Extra Shows

In the early 1970s, there were not as many orchestral concerts as today. Hence, the twelve symphonic concert programmes were each performed three times. Due to popular demand, some programmes were given a fourth or even fifth performance. Conversely, some programmes did not sell well, but still had to be played three times. There were twenty-eight programmes in the 2024/25 season. Normally, a programme is performed on Friday and Saturday. Some special programmes are performed once or three times.

Setbacks

Apparently, planning for the 1974/75 season was not thorough enough (some programmes and soloists were not confirmed when the subscription was launched). Quite a few works and artists had to be replaced. Popular Japanese violinist Takako Nishizaki stood in for English pianist

John Ogdon for the concerts from 16 to 18 August 1974 and shared the stage for the first time with HK Phil under the direction of Lim Kek-tjiang. That occasion was a milestone in her association with Hong Kong.

Photo 29.1: Leaflet of the Tenth Anniversary Lucky Draw. Grand prize: a pair of tickets to hear Herbert von Karajan conducting Berlin Philharmonic in Tokyo in 1984. Courtesy of Tseng Sun-man.

Everyone Knows These Subscribers

Nevertheless, the 1974/75 subscription had a remarkable launch. The audience response was not bad. At the very least, there were two familiar names – Sir Murray and Lady MacLehose – among the blue series subscribers. You are right: that was the governor and his wife.

The Lucky Subscriber and the Super Prize

It is common for subscribers to receive a gift. The incentive for the 1984/85 season was ground-breaking and will never happen again!

General Manager John Duffus loved to go to Japan. During one excursion there, he learned that Karajan would soon lead the Berlin Philharmonic to perform in Tokyo. An idea came to his mind! He quickly approached the concert organiser to buy a pair of tickets at a discounted rate. Then he approached Cathay Pacific, inviting them to donate a flight, hotel plus breakfast package. Subscribers to the 'Gold

Series' were allowed to take part in a lucky draw to win the super prize.

The lucky subscriber Ms Amy Yung and her friend took a flight to Tokyo and watched the Berlin Philharmonic and Karajan in action on 21 October 1984. They were thrilled. At Narita Airport, and in front of a Cathay Pacific airplane, a photo was taken of them wearing the HK Phil T-shirt, and looking spirited.

Photo 29.2: Accompanied by a friend, the lucky subscriber Ms Amy Yung (right) took a flight to Tokyo for an enviable concert experience.

Assistant General Manager (Development and Marketing) Tseng Sun-man went on the same tour. All costs were out of his own pocket. Forty years later, when asked why he did so, he said it was partly because it was a golden opportunity to see Karajan live, and partly because he wanted to ensure that particular HK Phil subscription initiative was properly recorded. Photo 29.2 at the airport was indeed taken by him.

30 *Moments of Sentiment*

HK Phil makes music that traverses a full range of feelings. Let us have a glimpse of members' different sentiments too.

Happily Ever After

On one occasion, everyone in the concert hall was electrified. On 25 February 2023, Principal Tuba Paul Luxenberg had just finished playing the John Williams concerto. He returned to stage with a unique encore – a live proposal. Everyone was caught by surprise, and even fellow musicians had not known about it. Paul kept the secret well! Amid cheers, blessings, laughter, and clapping, she said yes! A little update: on 3 April 2025, at a rehearsal, Paul told me that they already have a toddler, with another little one coming in summer. Congratulations!

Tension

Some said conductor Arrigo Foa had a quick temper. Michael Corp was a young National Service officer in the Royal Engineers. He was also an oboist in the pre-professional HK Phil. He recalled one day in September 1960: on a first play through of the Overture from *Nabucco*, players did not pick up on the rhythms and Italian subtleties of Verdi's music (Foa was Italian). The conductor screamed and the baton flew over the heads of musicians, breaking against the back of St. John's Hall. Dead silence followed. Solomon Bard put his violin down and followed Arrigo out. He did return with a grin on his face, but the rehearsal was abandoned.

HK Phil's days are full of joy too!

Farewell Drink

In recent years, the orchestra has established a tradition of ending a concert season with a drinks party. Chief Executive Timothy Calnin once made one hundred glasses of martini backstage! Sometimes the party takes place at a bar nearby. While celebrating another successful year, everyone also exchanges wishes for a happy summer break.

HK Phil Defeats London Phil

Sports bring happiness! The HK Phil football team has quite a happy record. In 2008, they beat London Philharmonic Orchestra (LPO) in a competitive game, 6–5. The scorers included Sebastian Jacot (flute), Wong Sze-hang (violin), Christopher Moyse (trumpet), and George Lomdaridze (double bass). The team also included Ni Lan (violin), Jonathan Clarke (trumpet), Jonathan Van Dyke (double bass), and Paul Luxenberg (tuba).

What would be more fun than playing against another orchestra? The answer: to play against more orchestras. The team did. They were defeated by Shanghai Opera in 2007, but just a few months before the LPO match, they beat Welsh National Opera!

Photo 30.1: HK Phil and LPO football teams.

Another gleaming achievement that the HK Phil football team holds is winning the championship of a local Hong Kong league a few times! Other than football, HK Phil's staff and players have also found pleasure in golf. In February 2008, Cheung Ming-yuen (cello), Steven Chan (stage manager), Ambrose Yeung (orchestra personnel manager), Ni Lan (violin), Christine Wong (violin), and Vance Lee (bassoon) competed in a friendly round of golf against the New York Philharmonic. HK Phil came second and NY Phil took third place. The championship went to another local team – the Discovery Bay Golf Club.

Photo 30.2: HK Phil players and staff enjoyed a friendly round of golf with NY Phil players.

On music and sports, Jonathan Van Dyke has an interesting thought:

> It was fascinating to observe other musicians on the field. Players often tend to take a similar role on the soccer field as on the stage. For example, I perform a supporting role as a tutti bassist; the ideal position for me in the HK Phil soccer team is defender! Other players who have more prominent roles in the orchestra tend to play more forward positions. Perhaps the same coordination and confidence that enables them to play such fantastic solos on stage also serve them to be nimble on the soccer field.

Drinking on Stage

Every year, after the final chord of the last piece of music is played at the Viennese New Year concert, players will hug and shake hands with each other. It is always a joyful moment. One year, someone brought in a champagne with glasses, and the delighted audience witnessed a drinking party on stage.

Encore Guests

Some soloists inject a bit of creativity in their encores. On 26 June 2021, after playing Mozart's Piano Concerto no. 26, 'Coronation', Colleen Lee returned to stage with conductor Lio Kuokman. Suddenly, the two of them sat down and began playing a movement from Mozart's Sonata K. 521 for piano four-hands.

Photo 30.3: Colleen Lee and Lio Kuokman.

Something similar happened at the 2023/24 season finale. Pianist Seong-Jin Cho and conductor Tarmo Peltokoski 'impulsively' brought to the audience the four-hand version of Brahms's Hungarian Dance no. 5.

Photo 30.4: Tarmo Peltokoski and Seong-Jin Cho.

On 23 December 2019, Hiromi was in the spotlight. In one of the encores, double bass player Jeffrey Lehmberg lifted up his enormous instrument, squeezed his way through the cello section, and started jamming with the jazz diva, much to the audience's delight.

Photo 30.5: Hiromi and Jeffrey Lehmberg.

The above three encores brought the house down!

Mrs Simon's Glory

For Principal Clarinet Andrew Simon, time stood for a moment at the 2018 Swire Symphony Under the Stars concert. He was ready to play the ethereal Adagio from the Mozart concerto when the emcee Harry Wong suddenly told the crowd of 18,000 that Andrew's mom had travelled all the way from the United States to watch the show. He invited Mrs Simon to stand up while enjoying her son's performance. The audience was thrilled, and those around Mrs Simon started giving her champagne and chocolates. Some fifteen people took a selfie with the proud mom.

Photo 30.6: Mrs Simon.

The story continues . . .

Andy was very happy to learn that a photograph of his mother, which he had previously shared with me, was to be included in HK Phil's fiftieth anniversary book (Chinese version). In March 2024, a few days before the books were printed, he sent me a voice message from his home in the United States, telling me that his mother was quite frail, and wondered if I could send him that particular page so he might show it to her. To my great relief, he was able to do so shortly before she passed away.

When he returned to Hong Kong, his next major assignment was to play the Mozart concerto again. In light of his mother's condition, the orchestra had offered to postpone the performance. However, Mrs Simon told Andy that she would rather he played the piece in remembrance of her, if she should pass. Andy did play it as scheduled (incidentally, on the book's launch day), and dedicated that beautiful performance to the memory of his mother.

A couple of months later, there was an auction at HK Phil's 50th Anniversary Dinner. When Andy found out that one of the auction items was sponsoring the publication of the English version of the book, he was determined to make it happen. This book might not have come into existence without his generous sponsorship, and I am deeply touched that this publication is one born out of love.

Grief

Nanking! Nanking!

If listeners are moved by a piece of music, players – who have listened over and over to the same work (at least at rehearsals) – may feel its sentiment even more.

In 2003, the orchestra recorded *Nanking! Nanking! A Threnody for Pipa and Orchestra* – a piece Bright Sheng wrote in memory of the victims of the Nanking Massacre. Before the recording session, the composer explained to players how he portrayed the horrors of the massacre, and depicted, for example, the sound of gunshots in the piece. After recording, it took some time for players to settle their emotions.

That's What Friends Are For

To perform and record Wagner's *Ring* was a huge challenge. Behind the scenes, a lot of groundwork had to be done too – including the ordering of music scores.

A serious problem emerged at the first rehearsal of *Das Rheingold*. There were only rehearsal letters (A, B, C etc.), but no bar numbers on the players' part scores. The conductor's score was the opposite. There were no rehearsal letters, but only bar numbers. With that scenario, it would be hard for Jaap to indicate where to start. Eventually, that rehearsal was dismissed.

Betty Ho, the orchestra's librarian, was most stressed: 'It is not possible to re-order the parts. How about I write all the bar numbers onto each part score? There are however, 3,900 bars in total, and eighty desks! This is mission impossible! The next rehearsal will happen tomorrow. What to do?'

That evening, a large group of colleagues and some of Betty's friends stayed at the office until midnight to copy bar numbers onto each part score.

Looking back after ten years, Betty is still extremely thankful: 'This deep-rooted friendship drives me to keep working hard.'

In Loving Memory

18 December 2018 was a tragic day. There was a short brush-up session before the concert, and everyone was at the Cultural Centre Concert Hall early. Suddenly, the voice of Raff Wilson, director of artistic planning, was heard over the backstage and dressing room PA system, calling members of the players' committee to gather in the conductor's room for a special discussion. Soon, all players were seated quietly on stage. Breaking the silence, Chief Executive Michael MacLeod told everyone about the sudden passing of Orchestra Personnel Manager Ambrose Yeung.

Everyone vividly remembered Ambrose reminding everyone to come to the brush-up rehearsal after the morning rehearsal. Before the concert, there was a break for a few hours, and Ambrose went for a badminton game with some players. On the way back, he suffered a fatal heart attack in his car.

Ambrose had cultivated an interest in music since he was young. His association with HK Phil started very early. As a secondary school student, he joined the Friends of the Philharmonic. After finishing his studies overseas, Ambrose returned and joined the orchestra as a full-time staff member.

Colleagues have fond recollections of Ambrose. He was helpful, and his face always seemed to radiate sunshine. He left Co-Principal Trumpet Christopher Moyse with particularly sweet memories. When first arriving in Hong Kong, Chris heard a knock on his hotel room door – and it turned out to be that amiable young guy. Ambrose helped him buy an Octopus card, showed him where the nearest Wellcome supermarket was, took him to his first HK Phil lunch, and brought him to Cheung Sha Wan to get a Hong Kong identity card. That extra mile that Ambrose went made him a Hong Kong ambassador to Chris.

On hearing the news, performers, office staff members, and stage crew who had worked shoulder-to-shoulder with Ambrose for years gathered backstage. The place was filled with tears, sighing, and an air of heavy sadness.

A tough question followed. Given the shock of the news, was it appropriate to let musicians play while they were in such unsettled emotional state? Some took another view: that the show must go on. Finally, Music Director Jaap van Zweden decided to cancel the concert, a decision which was well respected by the audience. The concert on the second night went ahead as planned.

Many friends, colleagues at HK Phil, and those within the arts circle attended Ambrose's funeral. Players formed a string quartet and played some of his favourite classical tunes at the ceremony.

A Musical Life

Bass trombone player Pieter Vance Wyckoff was diagnosed with brain cancer in March 2018. He was a fighter and was determined to combat the sickness. Y. S. Liu, chairman of the Board of Governors, personally lent him US$40,000 as downpayment for the surgery he required in the United States. The money was repaid when he obtained his insurance compensation. After surgery, Pieter returned to work. Colleagues were moved by his determination and will power.

Unfortunately, his health subsequently declined. Players and colleagues often went to visit him in hospital. A few players even created a roster, taking turns to care for him and feed him.

While in hospital, Pieter would pick up his trombone to play – the mark of a truly dedicated musician. During his final days, when he lay unconscious in bed, a colleague brought him a mouthpiece. Pieter started buzzing on it, a conditioned reflex which showed how inseparable he was from his instrument, his lifelong companion.

PVW Brain Tumor Foundation

Pieter Vance Wyckoff passed away on 14 June 2019 but left a humanitarian cause behind. A few colleagues established the PVW Brain Tumor Foundation to raise awareness of brain cancer and help patients. Earlier in the year on 21 May, at the foundation's inaugural concert, HK Phil players took part in a private capacity to perform Brahms's music – Pieter's favourite.

All You Need Is Love

There is much love and compassion among HK Phil colleagues. It may not even matter how well they know each other.

One morning in the 1990s, the plane that carried the HK Phil touring troupe was on its way to Beijing. The general manager's secretary picked up the phone and heard a slightly shaky voice, 'Oh dear! I overslept! It will be too late to catch the plane . . .'

The secretary was concerned, and she started to pacify the player, 'Don't worry. Quickly go buy an air ticket. I will call up the general manager as soon as possible.'

'Thank you, but . . . I have no money!' (from apprehension to disappointment).

The secretary immediately dashed to the bank and drew money from her own account to help the gentleman, whom she might not even have met.

It was a narrow escape for the musician. He did not only return the money, but also expressed his heartiest appreciation towards the secretary.

Rest assured that this was not a case of telephone scamming!

The Pregnant Conductor

In March 1989, HK Phil held a public concert at Harbour City. A nurse passed by and stayed to watch the show. She noticed that the conductor was pregnant and that she was having to catch her breath when introducing the works. The next day, the nurse called up the orchestra's office to voice her concern. When Yip Wing-sie learned about this, she confirmed that she had already consulted her doctor, who had told her that at seven months' pregnant, she could still conduct.

Undoubtedly, this particular audience member did not only care about listening to the music, but also about the musicians' wellbeing.

All these years later, Yip Wing-sie would like to thank the dear nurse and tell her that Desmond, whom she was carrying, got married in January 2023.

31 *Silent Applause*

When a performance is finished, audience members clap in appreciation. Musicians also show their approbation, but in addition to applause, there may be other gestures.

Gently tapping one's own instrument is a sign of respect. String players hit their music stands with their bows for the same purpose (usually not forcefully, and more often just waving them, because bows are precious and delicate!). Once in a while, the concertmaster is reluctant to respond to the conductor's gesture to lead the whole orchestra to stand up. This is not an act of disrespect; on the contrary, it is to indicate that it is time for the maestro to step on to the podium again to acknowledge the applause.

Second Associate Concertmaster Wang Liang told me a little secret. Particularly in the case of wind players, they indicate their approval of a nearby colleague's solo playing with some small movements: gently rubbing the floor or lightly touching his/her own thigh. This 'silent applause' during a performance always makes the neighbouring musician very happy!

32 *The Bet*

Rehearsals can be stressful or boring; but at times, they can be fun! Here's another story that Wang Liang told me.

In June 2014, pianist Boris Berezovsky played Rachmaninov's *Rhapsody on a Theme of Paganini* in the orchestra's fortieth anniversary concert. Music Director Jaap van Zweden conducted.

At a rehearsal, Boris said, 'At bar twenty-eight in the fifteenth variation, the orchestral entry will not be together.'

The Music Director said firmly, 'No!'

Boris said, 'You want to bet on that!'

He took the last remaining HK$50 note from his pocket and put it on the piano. That moment in the music came and the orchestra's entry was perfect! The rehearsal went on. Jaap continued to conduct and quickly used his left hand to grab the banknote and put it into his own pocket.

When the piece was over, a big roar of laughter followed. Jaap said with a grin, 'This is how I make money!'

Wang Liang explained, 'That bar is classic. The piano has a long and fast cadenza. When the orchestra comes in, however, it is *pianissimo.* If the conductor does not pay close enough attention, that entry is doomed!'

33 *A Romantic Orchestra*

HK Phil plays a lot of romantic works. That, however, does not make it a romantic orchestra. Something else does.

Colleagues are good friends. When not rehearsing or performing, they enjoy meeting each other. Popular activities include hiking, boat trips, drinking, playing soccer, or cooking at someone's place.

Photo 33.1, Photo 33.2, and Photo 33.3: HK Phil players and administrative staff enjoying their leisure time.

It is difficult to say how close they are to each other. One statistical figure gives us an objective indication though!

Among the players, there are thirteen married couples. The number only includes full-time players. Freelancers are not counted; unmarried lovers are also excluded. Some of them were already married before joining the orchestra. That means they both had to pass the audition. Some had a crush on each other when they became fellow players. In this way, the orchestra was their matchmaker!

At present, HK Phil has ninety-six players. Putting it mathematically, one out of every 3.7 players have a colleague as a spouse! I guess one reason why this rate is so high is because HK Phil members' turnover rate has been low in recent years. Of course, it also shows that Cupid watches over the orchestra.

The thirteen couples are:

Ai Jin (first violin) – Lin Jiang (principal horn)

Gui Li (first violin) – Wang Liang (second associate concertmaster)

Marrie Rose Kim (oboe) – John Schertle (co-principal clarinet)

Lau Wai (clarinet) – Olivier Nowak (co-principal flute)

Damara Lomdaridze (viola) – George Lomdaridze (principal double bass)

Rachael Mellado (first violin) – Jarod Vermette (principal trombone)

Tae-mi Song (cello) – Lorenzo Iosco (associate principal bass clarinet)

Megan Sterling (principal flute) – Christian Goldsmith (trombone)

Linda Stuckey (associate principal piccolo) – James Boznos (principal timpani)

Miyaka Suzuki Wilson (second violin) – Michael Wilson (principal oboe)

Tomoko Tanaka (second violin) – Mao Yiguo (second violin)

Sophia Woo Suk-fai (percussion) – Homer Lee (horn)

Zhao Yingna (principal second violin) – Anders Hui (second associate concertmaster)

34 *When the Sky Isn't Blue*

While I was writing this chapter, Super Typhoon Saola was hitting Hong Kong, and a hurricane signal number 10 was issued.

How's the Weather?

The sky was not blue either on 29 July 1978. Typhoon Agnes was not as strong as Saola but was powerful enough to push HK Phil's concert to the following day. Nancy Loo was soloist in the Chopin Piano Concerto no. 1. She had no recollection of the rescheduling though.

Not surprising. After all, it is not uncommon for performance activities to be affected by severe weather conditions. Not just typhoons: ten days or so before Hong Kong's handover in 1997, it was cloudy and rainy. On the internet, one can still see the orchestra perform at Tamar. Transparent plastic sheets were used to wrap up the cellos. There were also extra 'players' on stage, carrying umbrellas for musicians!

Swire Symphony Under the Stars usually takes place in rather comfortable and dry weather. One year, it was exceptionally hot. Players had to take off their jackets while playing. Another year, it suddenly turned cold. The orchestra quickly sourced some tall infrared heaters (the type that is seen in outdoor restaurants) to be put on stage. In yet another year, it got really windy. Musicians struggled to clip their music scores, pick up loose manuscripts, and play from memory. It was embarrassing. The orchestra's librarian Betty had to dash onto the stage, crouch down in front of the conductor's music stand, and serve as Jaap's 'human paper clips'.

Water Music

There was a heavy downpour at the concert on 16 November 2024, and the show had to be cut short. Very short, in fact, with only the opening piece – Rimsky-Korsakov's *Dance of the Tumblers* from *Snow Maiden*, and the closing *1812 Overture* (the show began in snow, and ended in rain!!). Everyone seemed to be in good spirits though. First, the audience appreciated how the players and conductor Elim Chan kept going even under extremely unfavourable conditions. Second, players were amazed by the enthusiastic audience members, who bore with the late starting of the show and indicated no intention of leaving despite the torrential rain. Last but not least, the *1812 Overture* was, as usual, accompanied by sounds of cannons, extravagant lighting, and exuberant fireworks. This time, however, the beams of light were saturated with water! It was a splendid sight.

Photo 34.1: Swire Symphony Under the Stars in the rain on 16 November 2024.

More Unforeseeable Circumstances

Swire Symphony Under the Stars has not only been affected by adverse weather. In 2019, amidst social unrest, HK Phil made a public announcement, 'In the light of recent incidents and other unforeseeable circumstances, the HK Phil has decided to postpone Swire Symphony Under the Stars concert.'

In 2003, the orchestra had to cancel concerts because of SARS. The situation in 2019, however, was even more complicated. The orchestra had cancelled rehearsals, changed concert start time, skipped intervals, and even cut short a concert midway. There were lots of operational matters to deal with. According to Chief Executive Benedikt Fohr, however, when COVID-19 came in 2020, the challenges were much more serious.

Unceasing Cancellations and Uncertain Postponements

Concerts were unceasingly cancelled, and no one could tell if a postponed performance would really happen. Having said that, whether there would be a show or not, all groundwork had to be done. The first affected soloist was Rudolf Buchbinder. Originally, he was to perform on 31 January and 1 February 2020 and play the Beethoven piano concerto cycle in celebration of the composer's 250th anniversary. However, when he finally appeared in Hong Kong, it was September 2023, more than three-and-a-half years later! It was not Beethoven's year anymore. Yet the pianist still brought two of the composer's concertos to the local audience.

A World Premiere Missed

One programme that did not take place as scheduled featured Joe Hisaishi. The composer's Symphony no. 2 was supposed to be unveiled by HK Phil in December 2020. Unfortunately, the concert was postponed to June 2021 and subsequently cancelled. When the local audience finally got to hear the piece in June 2023, we had already missed Hisaishi's Hong Kong premiere.

Never Give Up

This new normal came with much hardship. Despite that, HK Phil soldiered on. No matter how big or small the venue was, or how many people there were in the audience, whenever there was a chance, the orchestra would stage a show. When no audience members were allowed, they played to an empty house for broadcast. When all concert venues were closed, they appeared outdoors in Central, Sai Kung, and inside the MTR (including train compartments). For the latter, from nocturnes to aubades, overnight shooting took place when train services took a break in the small hours. When no venue whatsoever was available, players opened their home as concert halls, continuing to deliver music through cyberspace.

Replacements

Many overseas performers were unable to come to Hong Kong. Instead, local artists including Colleen Lee, Rachel Cheung, Vanessa Wong, and HK Phil players such as Concertmaster Jing Wang and Principal Cello Richard Bamping stood in as soloists. The orchestra also made special arrangements with other concert presenters, allowing overseas artists who had finished quarantine to perform both as soloists with HK

Phil and as recitalists. Some performers found this arrangement more worthwhile. After all, it was not a pleasant experience to travel and get put in quarantine.

Running Out of Conductors

Some conductors who took the trouble to come to Hong Kong and go through quarantine were invited to direct more programmes. During COVID, Lio Kuokman and Wilson Ng had conducted HK Phil quite a few times. One time, Kuokman nearly missed the show. He was rejected for boarding because his PCR test did not comply with an airline's requirements. Luckily, at the last minute, another flight company was able to take him on.

To cope with the problem of not having enough conductors, players including Lorenzo Iosco, Domas Juškys, Leung King-fung, and Andrew Ling were given opportunities to display their talent in conducting.

Fly In → Quarantine → Fly Out

The pandemic was unpredictable. There were times when concert venues were open, and the prospect of staging concerts seemed promising. In October 2020, François-Frédéric Guy was scheduled to come to Hong Kong, go through a three-week quarantine, and perform the complete Beethoven piano concertos series. He usually conducts while playing, and that would have saved the orchestra the trouble of finding a conductor. However, COVID got more serious again, and regrettably the French pianist had to fly off. A similar case happened with Music Director Jaap van Zweden. It was demoralising indeed.

There were more problems to solve! HK Phil implemented many anti-COVID measures: string players each had their own desk, transparent acrylic partitions were set up between players, the number of players on stage was kept to a limit, and facemasks were worn. Many of us still have vivid memories of these scenes.

What about COVID testing? According to the orchestra, between 9 November 2020 and 18 December 2022, players (mostly unmasked wind players) took a total of 4,044 PCR tests. Those days were tough!

October 2020 was most likely the toughest. To HK Phil, the sky certainly was not blue; in fact, it was depressingly gloomy.

Penny's Bay

Conductor Lio Kuokman reminisces about that concert:

> The pandemic abated, and venues reopened. How exciting that we could give live concerts, and feel the support of a live audience! I chose to play Copland's *Fanfare for the Common Man*, and Doming Lam's *Thanks to Joe-Kwan* to pay tribute to medical staff, and the eminent Hong Kong composer respectively. Concertmaster Jing Wang and Principal Cello Richard Bamping teamed up with me in the Triple Concerto by Beethoven, whose 250th anniversary was to be celebrated.

Regretfully, a player tested positive. All players who took part in the concerts on 9 and 10 October had to go to Penny's Bay in Lantau Island for quarantine. Two players were pregnant, and some brought family members who needed care into the quarantine site.

During those ten days or so, some players practised on their instruments. Some enjoyed chats with colleagues next door. Everyone tried to discover a new style of living. The wife of double bass player Philip Powell is a clinical psychiatrist. She offered online face-to-face counselling service to players. To keep everyone healthy, contrabass bassoonist Adam Treverton Jones, who is a yoga coach, led colleagues in yoga sessions. The orchestra management also responded quickly. They helped supply players with resources and arranged delivery services. At the same time, the PR department had to deal with a lot of media enquiries.

Photo 34.2: HK Phil's Beethoven Triple Concerto concert led by Lio Kuokman.

With much hard work and endurance, the quarantine period was finally over. Then came the good news: no one was infected.

A Quarantine Record Breaker

During COVID, every time Lio Kuokman returned to Hong Kong, he had to quarantine. During those three years, in order to conduct HK Phil, he went through more than 180 days of quarantine. It was quite a record indeed.

The pandemic has brought about a new form of art – online singing or playing. HK Phil combined both, and made a large-scale contribution.

Below the Lion Rock

The orchestra chose to perform the famous *Below the Lion Rock*. This Cantonese song, which is known to many local people, exalts the Hong Kong spirit: the determination to overcome adversity. More than 130 people took part in the virtual performance. The driving orchestral part was played by individual musicians. Voices from HK Phil's Board of Governors, management team, HK Phil Chorus, Club Bravo, Young Audience Scheme, and the Hong Kong Children's Choir were heard. Another supporter was the orchestra's longtime partner, singer/composer/producer Anthony Lun. Non-Chinese participants in the singing part included Chief Executive Benedikt Fohr and Director of Artistic Planning Timothy Tsukamoto. The orchestration was done by tenor Alex Tam, who also took part in singing. Editor Cheung Wai-lok performed the daunting task of putting more than 100 video clips together.

The video is still available online. Performances were mostly recorded in participants' homes (some were in home clothes), piano studios, offices and rehearsal rooms. Hong Kong landmarks – Victoria Harbour and Lion Rock – also appeared. Everyone gave their best. More than that, some of them held printed messages or slogans to cheer for Hong Kong. This video of less than four minutes represents a collective effort from HK Phil and friends, to express a message of 'love, caring and sharing'.

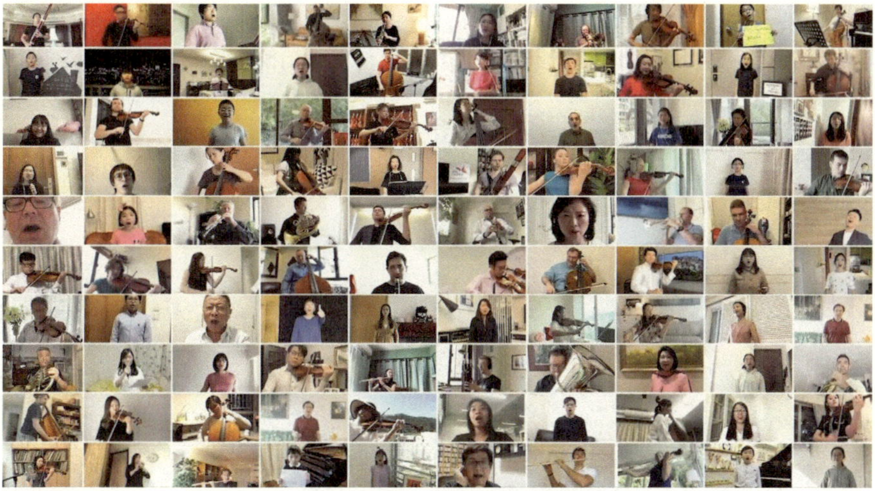

Photo 34.3: *Below the Lion Rock* virtual performance.

More HK Phil Online

During COVID, especially when the pandemic was serious, many people were forced to stay at home. This brought considerable stress. HK Phil was convinced that beautiful music soothes the soul, and services on HK Phil's website were enriched with innovative content. On the 'Watch and Listen' page, there were a lot of free concerts including the orchestra's appearance at Musikverein, Vienna, and recent performances in which players and audience members were seen wearing facemasks.

On top of concerts, the orchestra produced down-to-earth programmes such as Music × Food. The orchestra's cellist Anna Kwan visited a kitchen, and Second Associate Concertmaster Wang Liang was a customer in a restaurant. They chatted with the chef and the restaurant owner respectively. Their conversations covered both culinary topics and music. Anna and Liang looked like professional TV hosts.

Of course, their professionalism in music was also on full display when they played their instruments in the kitchen and dining hall.

Photo 34.4 and Photo 34.5: Music × Food programme featuring Anna Kwan (cello) and Wang Liang (second associate concertmaster).

In Music × Wellness, members of the orchestra's string quartet attended a yoga class led by an instructor before playing Haydn. Not sure if the class brought more vibes to the music?

Fun Phil Tong Chong Street was a delightful episode. Musicians dressed casually and presented a fusion version of Paganini's Caprice no. 24 on the laid-back Tong Chong Street in Quarry Bay. Passersby were subtly invited to swing their bodies to the music.

For parents and children, there were story-time videos and clips that introduced the four families of orchestral instruments.

The Ring for Free

The orchestra got a green light from Naxos to put their recording of Wagner's *Ring* cycle online for free listening: the full fourteen-hour-

and-fifty-five-minute recording, which took four years to make. Listeners were literally becoming at home with Wagner's music.

Heartwarming Moments

Even the toughest of times must end. Upon the easing of pandemic restrictions, Hong Kong gradually recovered in 2023. The orchestra also resumed its performance and promotional activities. Joe Hisaishi finally returned. After a break of two years, the subscription scheme resumed, and Benedikt Fohr gladly announced on stage that the response to the 2023/24 season was a record high.

So goes the saying, 'Every grey cloud has a silver lining.' Looking back, during those challenging three years, there were plenty of heart-warming moments.

There were so many cancellations, postponements, and re-postponements! When the orchestra's ticketing officer was busy with refunding work, some audience members expressed their support and asked the ticketing office to withhold a refund, hoping that the concert would eventually take place. When a show really had to be called off, some ticket holders chose to make the money a donation to HK Phil.

Another heartwarming moment happened at a special online Father's Day concert. It was an empty hall but filled with family love!

Principal Viola Andrew Ling came onto the stage with his son Gabriel, who appropriately began the concert by reciting *Pour mon père* ('For my Father') – a poem by Maurice Carême. He then sat down on stage to watch his father play. Another violist Ni Lan was in a string duo with his son Jayden, who played the cello. Principal Oboe Michael Wilson teamed up with Charlie (recorder) and Oliver (cello). The father-and-son trio became a quintet with the addition of two colleagues: Aziz D. Barnard Luce (principal percussion) and Jeffrey Lehmberg (double bass). Third Horn Homer Lee's family trio comprised of his wife Sophia

Woo (percussion) and son Yannis (piano). Cellist Chan Ngat-chau was accompanied on the piano by his daughter Adele. Rounding off the concert was a family quartet made up of Principal Timpani James Boznos, his daughter Zoë (ukelele), and sons Alexander (drums) and Harrison (trumpet).

Photo 34.6: Andrew and Gabriel Ling performed as a father-and-son duo. The pianist was Linda Yim.

Amidst a time of social distance, it was especially blissful to witness family members staying close to each other and making music together.

The Stranded Trumpeter

A story with a twist happened during the pandemic. In September 2021, Nitiphum Bamrungbanthum came all the way from Thailand, did two weeks of quarantine, and started two weeks of trial as principal trumpet. The pandemic posed challenges for air travel; while he found himself stranded in Hong Kong, the orchestra also needed an accomplished player to fill the vacancy. As a happy coincidence, his trial was extended for three months and further extended till the end of the season. In September 2022, he was offered a probation year for the position. It did not take that long though; in February 2023, he got the full-time contract as principal trumpet.

Epilogue

Three days after I finished writing the Chinese version of this chapter, Hong Kong was met with a once-in-500-years super-heavy rainstorm. The morning rehearsal of the 2023/24 Season-Opening Concert was cancelled. The evening concert was rescheduled to the following day at 3 p.m. The orchestra responded quickly and efficiently. The originally full house ended up at around 60% capacity. The evening show, which was also a full house, began as scheduled at 8 p.m., meaning that the orchestra, conductor Jaap van Zweden, and soloist Joshua Bell had to play the programme twice within a few hours.

Incidentally, Jaap's knee was injured, and he had to be seated while conducting.

What's more, on 5 September 2024, for two years in a row, the season's opening concert was affected by adverse weather conditions. Typhoon Yagi postponed the first night to the following afternoon; incidentally, also at 3 p.m.

The sky really isn't always blue!

Even if the sky is blue, it does not mean everything will be okay. In 2024, when international travel was gradually becoming normal, the orchestra was scheduled to take to the sky from Singapore to Berlin. However, because of a strike at Lufthansa, the flight which all 100+ staff and musicians were going to take was cancelled. This happened abruptly. One can imagine how stressful it was, to have to move so many people from Asia to Europe within a short span of time. A quick solution was devised: the troupe was divided into ten small groups. All ten flights, one direct and nine via London, Paris, Zurich, Frankfurt, Helsinki, Frankfurt, and Dresden, reached Berlin on time. Only two suitcases were lost, but thankfully, both were later recovered. Phew!

35 *Philip's Fanfare*

For years, Philip Kwok was a key member of HK Phil's General Committee. Looking back, he feels glad to have witnessed the orchestra expand from around sixty-something to ninety-something members. He also initiated and helped set up the HK Phil's Endowment Fund.

Photo 35.1: Philip Kwok

When asked about how he sees the relationship between the committee and the orchestra, he answered, 'Give them a free hand to manage the orchestra.' Having said that, when HK Phil faced crisis, he would come forward to help with no hesitation.

When the Urban Council was abolished in 1999, the government's support of HK Phil was cut significantly. Hong Kong was yet to emerge from the Asian financial crisis. The economy was volatile. The orchestra had to do something! At a rehearsal, on the podium was not the conductor. It was Philip, chairman of the General Committee. Awkward feelings return when he recalls that moment, 'There was profound insecurity in the air when all eyes were on me! I told them, you will continue to receive your pay cheques.'

To Philip, it is sweet memory to have journeyed with the orchestra. He is thankful that music has put him into a position to serve. In fact, music was his farewell gift too. To celebrate the completion of his ten-year tenure as chairman of the committee (1981–1991), David Gwilt, who was his longtime colleague at the committee, wrote a piece especially for him. *Philip's Fanfare* was subsequently given its world premiere by the orchestra.

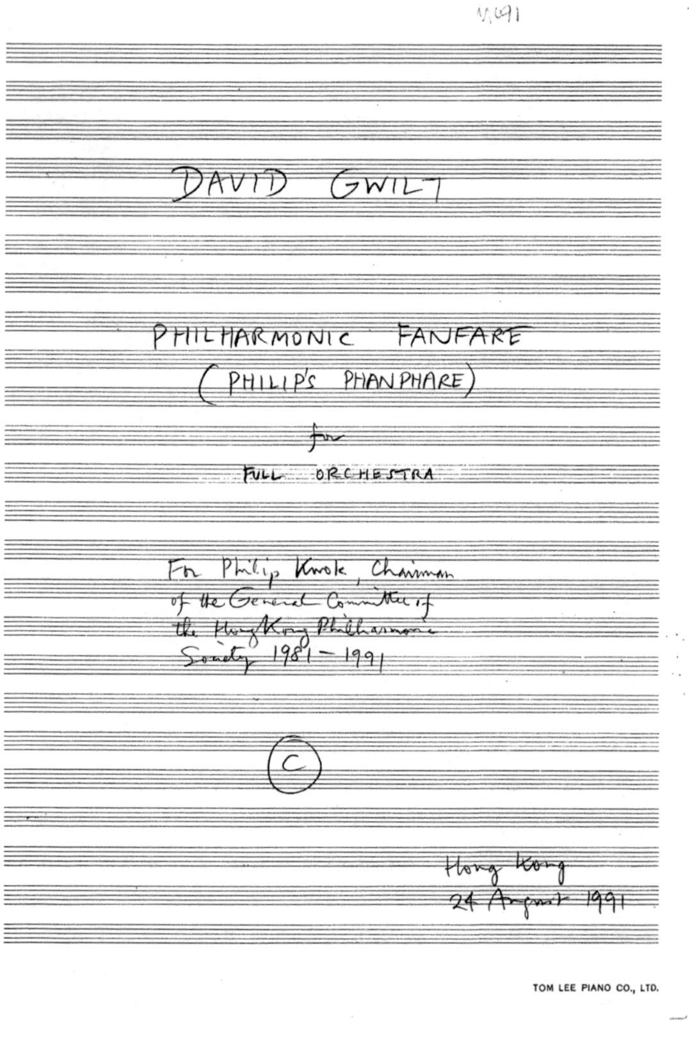

Photo 35.2: Manuscript of *Philip's Fanfare* by David Gwilt.

36 *Hello, Nínhăo, Kamusta, Annyeonghaseyo*

It was HK Phil's first trip to China in 1986. Musicians were waiting outside the venue where the Hangzhou concert was to begin soon. An audience member nearby asked the players, 'Is this an orchestra from the United Nations?'

This question puts the composition of HK Phil's membership into perspective.

For almost 200 years, Hong Kong has been attractive to people of different origins and nationalities. Some choose to stay briefly; others raise their families here and make Hong Kong home. One way or another, an international city is built.

Three Jewish Musicians

With robust population flows, many talented musicians were also brought in. From the 1920s to 1950s, three Jewish musicians came to Hong Kong and became closely associated with SBO. Harry Ore was born in Latvia and attended St. Petersburg Conservatory. Prior to making Hong Kong home, Solomon Bard had lived in Siberia, Harbin, and Shanghai. Arrigo Foa came from Italy, having worked in Shanghai before migrating to Hong Kong.

An International Cast

SBO had an international cast. Anthony Braga served as SBO's secretary for a long time. He and his pianist sister Caroline were of Portuguese decent. Their family had lived in Hong Kong and Macau for generations. Alastair Blair-Kerr was an SBO violinist who sometimes served as concertmaster. The Scottish judge's name became known to many when he took charge of the Peter Godber corruption case. Another violinist, Moya Rae, was a distinguished pianist too. She came from New Zealand with her husband, who worked at Taikoo Dockyard. One of the founders of the Sino-British Club, London-born Betty Drown helped prepare programme notes for SBO. She was a notable piano teacher whose students included Nancy Loo and Mary Wu.

Of course, SBO had many Chinese members, including Domingo Lam (violin), Wong Ching-kuen (flute), Chang Wing-sou (oboe and bassoon), Cheng Chik-pui (violin), Lo King-man (horn), and Frank Huang (cello, and a famous singer too). There were also players of other nationalities including Filipinos. 'Sino-British' may not have been the most accurate description.

Photo 36.1: In 1956, upon invitation by a cultural and arts organisation in Southern China, some SBO members visited Guangzhou for a performance. Courtesy of Jim Chang.

Photo 36.2 (above): Wong Ching-kuen (flute) and Chang Wing-sou (bassoon) in a duo performance. Courtesy of Jim Chang.
Photo 36.3 (right): Soprano Barbara Fei and pianist Harry Ore. Courtesy of Jim Chang.

Photo 36.4 (above): Anthony Braga.
Photo 36.5 (right): Betty Drown teaching a young student.

Photo 36.6: Lo King-man. Courtesy of Lo King-man.

The East–West mix continued. In 1968, HK Phil celebrated its twenty-first anniversary (counting from the founding of its predecessor SBO). In the programme, Solomon Bard had this to say, 'In the meantime the Hong Kong Philharmonic Orchestra stands today as Hong Kong's own orchestra, one of the more notable examples of cooperation between men and women of different races, creeds, and social backgrounds, all linked by one common interest – making music.'

Many local musicians of different backgrounds joined the professional HK Phil in 1974. On top of that, the first music director Lim Kek-tjiang (himself an Indonesia-born Chinese) travelled around Asia for auditions, and applications from other places were also considered.

There is a description in the 1974/75 subscription brochure:

> The 'new' Hong Kong Philharmonic will be the most international orchestra of any major city in the world. Musicians from the major Korean orchestras, the National Symphony and the Seoul Philharmonic Orchestra, will play alongside former members of the Manila Symphony Orchestra. And musicians who are now playing in major Japanese orchestras will join Americans who have played in orchestras such as the Cleveland Orchestra and Chicago Symphony Orchestra, the Dallas Symphony Orchestra, the Philadelphia Orchestra and a few minor American orchestras.

More Than Half Full-timers from Overseas

An Urban Council report dated 24 November 1973 detailed where the twenty-two overseas musicians came from. There were thirteen Koreans, three Filipinos, three Americans, two Japanese, and one French. One violinist was assistant concertmaster of KBS Symphony Orchestra. The three Filipino musicians were respectively principals in the flute, oboe and double bass sections of the Manila Symphony Orchestra. Locally, twelve musicians started working full-time for the new HK Phil.

A diverse mix of nationalities and ethnicities has continued to be one of HK Phil's prevailing features. In the 1990s, more British musicians joined.[1] In recent years, there have been more members from continental Europe.

As of late, HK Phil's makeup has included more local members. For example, in the woodwind section, Kwan Sheung-fung (associated principal cor anglais), Lau Wai (clarinet), and Toby Chan (co-principal bassoon) were born and musically trained in Hong Kong.

The Hong Kong Edge

A number of orchestras in nearby cities also have memberships of an international mix. Some players attribute the unique internationality of HK Phil to Hong Kong's geographical and cultural advantages, as well as infrastructures.

To those who come from the Chinese mainland, Korea, Japan, or Southeast Asia, working in Hong Kong means that it is easy for them to visit their homelands and see their families. Hong Kong is an international city, English is spoken by many, and there is a wide range of food options available – not to mention that Hong Kong's tax system is simple.

1 Among the twelve new members in the 1990/91 season, seven were British.

Before coming to Hong Kong, Concertmaster Jing Wang was in the same post at the orchestra of Dallas Opera. He said, 'I am sick of commuting. Hong Kong has one of the world's most convenient transport systems. One does not have to drive for three hours for a concert.' On the contrary: after a tiring rehearsal, in less than an hour one can chill out on a beach or at a country park. Despite occasional typhoons, the weather is mild. These are all attractive factors to expatriate musicians. No wonder many of them choose to be Hongkongers. In fact, many of them own properties here.

Although players speak different languages, there is one thing in common – they all communicate with each other, and the audience, in one international language – music! Except for that time . . .

Happy New Year!

On one occasion, one by one, some ten players used their native languages to wish everyone a Happy New Year. It was at the 2004 New Year Concert conducted by Edo de Waart. The final *xin nian kuai le* was delivered in loud and clear Putonghua by Principal Oboe Huang Zheng.

37 *Jaap's Asian Connections*

Jaap van Zweden became HK Phil's music director in 2012. Since then, we see him a lot at Cultural Centre. In fact, he was here on 5 and 6 September 1993 in another role. He was on tour as a concertmaster of the Royal Concertgebouw Orchestra.

In 2024, he was made Seoul Philharmonic's music director. In 2025, he became artist-in-residence with the Evergreen Symphony Orchestra in Taiwan. Looks like Asia is close to his heart!

Actually, his Asian connections started even earlier. His great-grandfather had lived in Indonesia. Mr van Zweden senior married an Indonesian-Chinese woman and moved back to the Netherlands. Hence, the conductor has some Asian heritage.

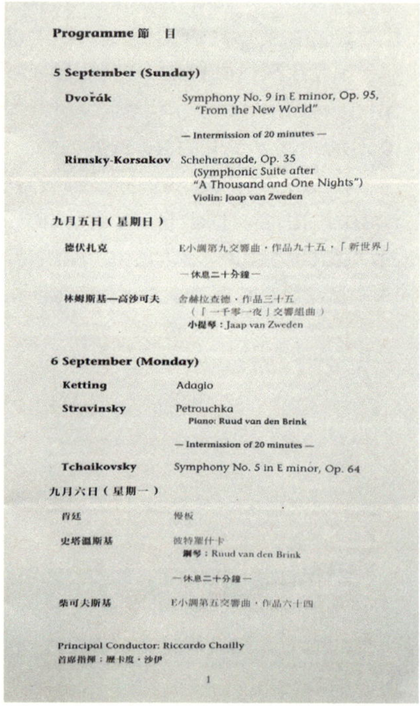

Programme 節 目

5 September (Sunday)

Dvořák Symphony No. 9 in E minor, Op. 95, "From the New World"

— Intermission of 20 minutes —

Rimsky-Korsakov Scheherazade, Op. 35 (Symphonic Suite after "A Thousand and One Nights")
Violin: Jaap van Zweden

九月五日（星期日）

德伏扎克 E小調第九交響曲・作品九十五・「新世界」

—休息二十分鐘—

林姆斯基—高沙可夫 舍赫拉查德・作品三十五（「一千零一夜」交響組曲）
小提琴：Jaap van Zweden

6 September (Monday)

Ketting Adagio

Stravinsky Petrouchka
Piano: Ruud van den Brink

— Intermission of 20 minutes —

Tchaikovsky Symphony No. 5 in E minor, Op. 64

九月六日（星期一）

肯廷 慢板

史塔溫斯基 彼特羅什卡
鋼琴：Ruud van den Brink

—休息二十分鐘—

柴可夫斯基 E小調第五交響曲・作品六十四

Principal Conductor: Riccardo Chailly
首席指揮：裡卡度・沙伊

1

Photo 37.1 and Photo 37.2: In the first concert of the Royal Concertgebouw Hong Kong visit in 1993, Jaap van Zweden was the violin soloist in Rimsky-Korsakov's *Scheherazade*. Courtesy of Eric Li.

38 *Filemon's Hong Kong Love Song*

Hailing from the Philippines, music brought Filemon Corpus to Hong Kong; and from then, his life became a Hong Kong love song.

In 1959, while a player with the Manila Symphony Orchestra, the 36-year-old violinist decided to pursue his career in Hong Kong. He came over to get things settled first. Shortly after, his wife and son, little Ernesto, left the Philippines to reunite with him. A few years later, Aurora was born in Hong Kong. At first, Filemon played in hotels. He was a musician at Gaddi's at Peninsula and a band member at the Hilton. His talent was discovered by Solomon Bard, who invited Filemon to join the pre-professional HK Phil. In 1976, two years after the orchestra became a professional body, he was signed as a full-timer; he stayed until retirement in 1991.

Photo 38.1: Filemon was a member of the pre-professional to professional HK Phil. Courtesy of Ernesto Corpus.

In addition to playing at the HK Phil, because Ernesto studied at La Salle College, the professional parent also taught the violin at the school and became its music director.

Ernesto and Aurora recall, 'Father took pride in being part of the orchestra. He especially enjoyed going on tour. He would play jazz on planes. As a born comedian, he always brought a good laugh to people around him. One time, the featured soloist in a HK Phil tour was the violin diva Ida Haendel. Father was thrilled to be in the same frame with his idol.'

Photo 38.2: Filemon taking a picture inside a plane with Ida Haendel. Courtesy of Ernesto Corpus.

Raised in a household of music, Ernesto also became a musician. He frequently collaborated with the orchestra in pop concerts as pianist and arranger, sharing the stage with Frances Yip, Roman Tam, and Anthony Lun, who was his classmate at La Salle.

On countless occasions, Ernesto was in the audience watching his father play in the orchestra. In 2008, Lea Salonga worked with HK Phil for the first time. Originally, Ernesto planned to buy a ticket and bring his retired dad to see the show that featured the Filipina diva. The concert's conductor, Lea's brother Gerard, suddenly called Ernesto and asked if he would like to be the pianist at the concert. As it turned out, the proud father was in the audience as Ernesto shared the stage with Lea, Gerard, and the orchestra!

Music brought Filemon to Hong Kong where he made his home. His son and daughter also became musicians (Aurora is a singer who has appeared in leading roles in local musical productions). Having lived through fruitful years as a performer and teacher, Filemon passed away in 2011.

Filemon also took part in recording soundtracks for local movies. One love song which he has left us is *Evening Breeze* (from the 1984 movie *Shanghai Blues*), sung by Sally Yeh. That brilliant opening solo in the soundtrack was played on the violin by Filemon.

39 *Pop Goes the Phil*

A milestone was reached in the history of the orchestra from 3 to 6 September 1982. High-powered television executive Selena Chow was instrumental in lining up best-selling superstar Michael Kwan to perform with HK Phil at the Queen Elizabeth Stadium. The concerts were conducted by Joseph Koo, the Godfather of Cantopop. Annabelle Louie made a guest appearance. She had collaborated with Michael in a chart-topping duet, 人在旅途灑淚時 ('When Tears Are Shed on the Journey'), in 1980. In fact, they recorded their parts in studio separately. It was a truly rare occasion when the two appeared live on stage.

Photo 39.1: Poster of HK Phil's first pop concert featuring Michael Kwan in 1982.

The concerts' ticket sales, as well as the release of the live recording, were both highly successful. Another notable singer, Roman Tam, shared the stage with HK Phil at Sha Tin Racecourse in 1979 as a guest in that family programme. The rest of the programme was mainly classical. However, Michael Kwan set the precedent of combining the charm of a large-scale Cantopop concert with the very presence of Hong Kong's flagship orchestra.

Controversy

Having said that, this novel idea dismayed some lovers of classical music, who believed that HK Phil should not mix with pop. They were worried that this would affect HK Phil's 'tasteful image' and lower the orchestra's artistic standard. Some other felt that going pop should not be a means to build audience and increase income. The criticism went as far as comparing HK Phil to Faust selling his soul. Some other music-lovers (including classical fans), however, held an opposite view. They believed that this kind of collaboration could help redefine the 'high-brow' misconception that some people might have of HK Phil. Branching out into pop music meant more audiences would be able to feel the beauty of classical music. On the other hand, some had reservations about the processing and amplification of sound, fearing that the original colours and textures of orchestra music would be distorted. For a while, the discussion was heated.

At the concert in 1982, some classical music elements were incorporated into the programme. It was quite clear that one of the organiser's intentions was to promote 'serious' orchestral music.

Classical in Pop

The audience was treated to the main theme from *Star Wars*. On top of that, Michael displayed his talent on the classical side by playing Stanley Myers's *Cavatina* on the guitar, accompanied gently by the orchestra. This is not an easy piece, and he played really well. The tune was familiar to a great many, as it also appeared in the blockbuster *The Deer Hunter*. I wonder if that performance left a pleasurable impression of the classical guitar with Michael's fans in the crowd.

Butterfly Lovers Old and New

An excerpt of the *Butterfly Lovers' Concerto* appeared in the programme, partly because the tune had earlier been adapted in a pop song called 恨綿綿 ('Never-Ending Sorrow'). The arranger deliberately incorporated the flavour of the original concerto into the song. This version, which lasted about ten minutes, retained the opening cadenza on the flute, the prominent oboe solo, and a substantial part of the violin solo (played by the HK Phil's first associate concertmaster Benedict Cruft). The tune set to Cantonese, sung now by Michael, intertwined with the original music, while the audience had a taste of the concerto itself.

Photo 39.2: In 1996, Jacky Cheung was featured in Hongkong Bank Gold Cards Jacky and the Phil in Perfect Harmony to raise funds for the orchestra's Young Audience Scheme. This was a vivid example of pop for the benefit of the classical. The conductor was Yip Wing-sie.

In many pop concerts to follow, it became customary for the orchestra to include some classical pieces. Teresa Carpio's concert featured Mikhail Glinka's Overture from *Ruslan and Ludmila*; Frances Yip's concert incorporated Wagner's Prelude from *Die Meistersinger von Nürnberg*; Christopher Wong's concert included Massenet's 'Méditation' from *Thaïs* (violin solo: Leung Kin-fung); Sandy Lam and Anthony Lun's concert featured Copland's *Fanfare for the Common Man*; and Anthony Wong's concert incorporated 'Mars, the Bringer of War' from *The Planets* by Gustav Holst. David Atherton went a bit further. Once, he conducted a few classical works first before Yip Wing-sie took over the baton, joined by Frances Yip.

In retrospect, has participating in pop helped the orchestra reach new audiences? How many people have cultivated an interest in classical music while watching HK Phil's concerts? According to former assistant general manager (development and marketing) Tseng Sun-man, once the orchestra organised a concert of popular classics and offered a discount to those who had attended a specific pop concert. As it turned out, 5% of the audience subscribed to that classical concert. Notwithstanding this finding, it is still difficult to assess the correlation between the two. Is it right for an organisation with a mandate to promote classical music to raise funds by putting on pop concerts? It is not easy to find simple answers to such questions. A few things for sure: first, many people have had a chance to see an orchestra through attending a pop concert. Second, more people will come to know of the name 'Hong Kong Philharmonic Orchestra'. Third, musicians including players and conductors are exposed to musical styles such as jazz, Latin, Chinese, and electronic music. Fourth, the orchestra as a medium has served to inspire singers, arrangers, music directors, and conductors to further explore artistic possibilities.

What Are Those Possibilities?

Photo 39.3: For a moment, Wang Leehom was a conductor.

Some took advantage of the chance to realise their potential in performance on top of singing pop songs: Hins Cheung played the harp, Anthony Lun played the piano, and Faye Wong was a coloratura (who sang with Anthony Wong in *Phantom of the Opera* and reached an unforgettable high C – her name was Shirley then). As mentioned earlier, Michael Kwan played the classical guitar; Wang Leehom conducted and played the violin and pipe organ; and Ivana Wong composed music (at her concerts on 12 and 13 May 2023, the first half was purely her instrumental works).

The music featured at these concerts has consisted mainly of Chinese and Western pop songs. Sometimes there are folk songs and oldies. Often, works are new arrangements with a novel orchestral sound. The effect is quite different and occasionally experimental.

Photo 39.4: Ivana Wong × HK Phil 'The Missing Something' Concert sponsored by United Overseas Bank Limited.

Many singers have chosen to feature songs from musicals in their concerts. Priscilla Chan sang 'Don't Cry for Me Argentina', Frances Yip sang 'Send In the Clowns', and Teresa Carpio sang 'Could We Start Again Please?' In the world of pop, some songs are classically inspired – A-Mei sang Carmen (the Habanera from Bizet's *Carmen* was adapted into a popular Chinese oldie), and Justin Lo sang 'A Whiter Shade of Pale', which bears much resemblance to the Air from Bach's Orchestral Suite no. 3. Anthony Lun sang and played Barry Manilow's 'Could It Be Magic?' – a song that incorporates Chopin's Prelude no. 20.

Whose Voice?

Let us look at one technicality of a pop concert. Aside from the orchestra, pop music calls for a band (or the rhythm section), which includes instruments like electric keyboards, guitars, electric basses and drums. This combo often becomes the driving force of the music, sometimes to such an extent that the orchestra may sound secondary. In early years, some string players jokingly expressed that they enjoyed playing in a pop concert because the scores were full of long notes – a perfect opportunity for them to practise vibrato and changing positions.

That said, HK Phil has more than forty years of experience playing pop concerts. Musical professionals including arrangers, sound engineers and conductors have gathered much practical experience to help them utilise players' virtuosity in full. Concertmaster Jing Wang remembers very well the music arrangements made for the Hacken Lee concert: 'The orchestra did more than accompanying Hacken. We have a lot of interesting music to play.'

HK Phil 50 – Symphonic Reunion is a vivid example. With this latest pair of HK Phil pop concerts, the programme content was rich and presentation styles were varied. Music Director Harris Ho shared with me some highlights and thoughts behind the programming.

- The concert opened with Selina Chow making a speech. She briefly told the story of how she invited the orchestra to perform with Michael Kwan and unexpectedly opened a new chapter in the history of pop music in Hong Kong. She said some of Michael's songs, including 星 ('Star'), 一點燭光 ('Candle-Light') and 愛的音訊 ('Message of Love'; tune: Beethoven's *Ode to Joy*) fit well when sung with an orchestra. Harris chose 'Candle-Light' as the melody to accompany Selina's speech. It was most fittingly played on the violin by Jing Wang. This concert opener carried a special meaning: while Selina shared this story in words, the concertmaster told the same story with music.
- A medley of favourite classical tunes was heard. It included excerpts from Mozart's *Marriage of Figaro*, Wagner's *Ride of the Valkyries*, Bizet's *Carmen*, Tchaikovsky's *Romeo and Juliet Fantasy Overture*, Pachelbel's Canon in D, and 'Winter' from Vivaldi's *Four Seasons*; all in their original keys. It was a seamless transition from classical to pop: the final excerpt in F minor flowed smoothly into composer Joseph Koo's first successful song 夢 ('Dream') in A flat major (the relative major of F minor).
- In Elisa's song 今晚夜 ('Tonight'), there was a special section for the orchestra. In Harris's arrangement, each family of orchestral instruments, in the order of woodwind, percussion, strings and brass, was highlighted.
- Another medley arranged by Harris honoured the late composer Joseph Koo and lyricist James Wong. Koo and Wong collaborated in more than 200 songs. The arrangement subtly recapitulated the styles of orchestration in the 1970s and 1980s. For instance, the strings created a sound palette to back up the melodies; the woodwinds were highlighted in introductions and interludes; the brass played important roles in jazzy and funky passages; and percussion instruments such as the

timpani appeared prominently in theme songs of sword-fighting TV dramas. Harris said he also took care not to leave out the vibraslap – a percussion instrument of distinctive character used in the popular TV series 楚留香 ('Chor Lau Heung').

- A string octet made up of principals and associate principals from the orchestra's string sections accompanied Sandy Lam in 滴汗 ('Are You Ready for Love?').
- Frances Yip's most popular song is undoubtedly 上海灘 ('The Bund of Shanghai'). Joseph Koo had previously orchestrated a version for her and HK Phil, and that same version was heard again.
- A new generation of singers – Jay Fung, Oscar Tao, and Cloud Wan – took part in the concert, to signify the passing on of a tradition. They covered songs by singers George Lam, Hins Cheung, and Justin Lo –three gentlemen who have all been featured in previous HK Phil concerts.
- Johnny Yim saluted the local film industry with a HK movie medley. On screen, there were computer graphics of memorable scenes from blockbuster movies.
- Sandy Lam shared the stage with Anthony Lun, conductor Lio Kuokman, and Harris, who each played a piano. The music 微雨撲巴黎 ('Light Rain in Paris') was arranged by Joyce Cheung.
- The backing voices had a section on their own before joining Sandy. They did not just sing — they also danced!
- In tailcoats and evening gowns, twenty members of the HK Phil Chorus each held a microphone and sang in parts. This made for an impressive appearance.

The main objective of the production team was to recapitulate the essence of HK Phil's involvement with Cantopop while recognising the achievement made by singers and the orchestra collectively.

I found one scene particularly memorable. Danny Chan appeared with HK Phil at the 1983 Music Extravaganza – the orchestra's first show at Hong Kong Coliseum. Danny sadly passed away in 1993. He was only 35. AI technology was used to extract the vocal part from one of his early songs, 眼淚為你流 ('Tears for You'). The vocal track was played to live accompaniment by the orchestra (orchestration: Pong Law). While white confetti gently fell from the ceiling, it brought about a bittersweet feeling. I was overwhelmed with nostalgia remembering Danny singing at the same venue with the same orchestra forty-one years ago . . .

More Than Music

Double bass player Jonathan Van Dyke remarks on a non-music aspect of Hacken Lee's concert, 'Some artists know how to engage us. During the performances, videos were shown during Hacken's costume changes. He was filmed hanging out with HK Phil colleagues: Raymond Leung (percussion) hosted and cooked for Hacken at his place; Homer Lee (horn) and Sophia Woo (percussion) shared their love story; Andrew Ling (principal viola), and Nitphum Bamrungbanthum (principal trumpet) went for a foot massage with Hacken; and Jing Wang and Zhao Yingna (principal second violin) joined Hacken for wine-tasting and drinking games. After each video was shown, the next song in the show featured the players in that video. This engaged the audience on a different, more human level, and in turn we took more ownership of the show.'

One song occupies a special place in HK Phil's pop concert history. It was first heard by a live audience in March 1996.

HK Phil Tops the Pop Chart

Composer Lee Shih Shiong and lyricist Lin Xi co-presented a song as a wedding gift to Jacky Cheung and May Lo. After giving the world premiere of the song at one of the 'Hongkong Bank Gold Cards Jacky and the Phil in Perfect Harmony' concerts, the new bridegroom told the audience that the song did not even have a name yet. Subsequent to a light touch-up, 妳的名字我的姓氏 ('Your Name, My Surname') quickly swept the pop music scene. The version most widely heard in the media, and sung at karaokes, was the collaboration between Jacky and the HK Phil (conductor: Yip Wing-sie) recorded live. It topped pop charts in different parts of the world. This was Cantopop's new look. Does the full orchestral sound entice a new audience into the concert hall? To most people, it does not matter. One thing for sure, though: many listeners found this type of symphonic Cantopop especially appealing.

Photo 39.5 and Photo 39.6: After a break of sixteen years, the orchestra put on another pop concert at the Hong Kong Coliseum to mark HK Phil's fiftieth anniversary. Veteran artists Sandy Lam, Anthony Lun, Frances Yip, and Elisa Chan were joined by popular singers of the new generation – Jay Fung, Oscar Tao, and Cloud Wan – for two sumptuous evenings.

Finally, Table 39.1 lists concerts featuring pop singers

that the orchestra has organised or been involved with. While the spotlight generally falls on local singers, artists from other Chinese-speaking regions are included too.

Photo 39.7, Photo 39.8, and Photo 39.9: HK Phil has also shared the stage with a number of non-Chinese pop singers and bands including Secret Garden (2000), Laura Fygi (2005), and the Beach Boys (2016).

Table 39.1: HK Phil's pop concerts

Concert Title	Year and Venue	Conductor	Artist
Michael Kwan Live in Concert	1982 Queen Elizabeth Stadium	Joseph Koo	Michael Kwan Annabelle Louie as guest
Music Extravaganza	1983 Hong Kong Coliseum	Joseph Koo Yoshikazu Fukumura Doming Lam	Danny Chan Liza Wang Michael Kwan Johnny Yip Frances Yip
Top Pops of the '80s	1984 Hong Kong Coliseum	Yoshikazu Fukumura Michael Lai Hou Dejian	Leslie Cheung Anita Mui David Lui
A Splendid Philharmonic Night	1988 Hong Kong Coliseum	Yip Wing-sie	Anthony Lun Sandy Lam
Music Rendezvous	1991 Hong Kong Coliseum	Mak Ka Lok Yoshikazu Fukumura	Jackie Chan Lo Ta-yu Wakin Chau Jonathan Lee Anthony Wong Shirley Wong (later known as Faye Wong) Wa Wa and more
Music Lingers	1993 Hong Kong Coliseum	Yip Wing-sie	Wang Luobin Singers from Music Factory and more

New Love Song Era	1994 Hong Kong Coliseum	Yip Wing-sie	Jonathan Lee Lowell Lo Roman Tam Julie Sue and more
Symphony Under the Stars '94	1994 Happy Valley Racecourse	Yoshikazu Fukumura	Elisa Chan
Loving Love Songs	1995 Hong Kong Coliseum	Yip Wing-sie	Eric Moo Shirley Kwan Warren Mok
HongkongBank Gold Cards Jacky and the Phil in Perfect Harmony	1996 Hong Kong Coliseum	Yip Wing-sie	Jacky Cheung
First Pacific Bank Credit Card Musical Encounters with Priscilla & the Phil	1997 Hong Kong Coliseum	Yip Wing-sie	Priscilla Chan
The Phil & 4 Stars	1997 Hong Kong Coliseum	Yip Wing-sie	Kit Chan William So Joyce Lee Mark Lui
Frances Yip & The Phil '98 Simply the Best Concert	1998 Hong Kong Coliseum	David Atherton Yip Wing-sie	Frances Yip
HKPO & A-Mei Open Your Eyes 2000	2000 Hong Kong Coliseum	Yip Wing-sie	A-Mei

HKPO & Hacken	2001 Hong Kong Coliseum	Yip Wing-sie	Hacken Lee
HKPO & Alan Tam	2002 Hong Kong Coliseum	Yip Wing-sie	Alan Tam
Lam & HKPO Live 2002	2002 Hong Kong Coliseum	Choi Ho-man	George Lam
HKPO & Teresa Carpio DIVA	2003 Hong Kong Cultural Centre Shatin Town Hall	Choi Ho-man	Teresa Carpio
HKPO & Frances Yip DIVA	2004 Hong Kong Cultural Centre	Choi Ho-man	Frances Yip
HKPO Sandy × Anthony Live	2004 Hong Kong Coliseum	Choi Ho-man	Sandy Lam Anthony Lun
Sally Yeh HKPO Live Music in Motion	2005 Hong Kong Coliseum	Henry Shek	Sally Yeh
HKPO VS Anthony Wong Live Bauhinian Rhapsody	2006 Hong Kong Coliseum	Simon Kenway	Anthony Wong
HKPO × Chris Wong A Night to Remember	2006 Hong Kong Cultural Centre	Henry Shek	Chris Wong Guests: David Quah Vivian Chow
HKPO × Justin Live in Love with the Philharmonic	2007 Hong Kong Coliseum	Zhang Jiemin	Justin

HKPO Ronald Edmond Live	2008 Hong Kong Coliseum	Henry Shek	Ronald Cheng Edmond Leung
HKPO & Leehom Live	2008 Hong Kong Cultural Centre	Gerard Salonga	Wang Leehom
HKPO at the Movies with Elisa Chan	2010 Hong Kong Cultural Centre	Gerard Salonga	Elisa Chan
A Star in a Hall of Fame HKPO × Hins Cheung	2011 Star Hall, KITEC (Kowloon Bay International Trade & Exhibition Centre)	Gerard Salonga	Hins Cheung
Ivana Wong Fragrance of Music	2015 Hong Kong Cultural Centre	Gerard Salonga	Ivana Wong Guest: Alex Fung
Deanie Ip Anthony Lun Hei Chiu Hong Kong Philharmonic Orchestra Live 2016	2016 Hong Kong Convention and Exhibition Centre	Chiu Tsang-hei	Deanie Ip Anthony Lun
HK Phil × Anthony Lun The Man Behind the Piano Concert	2019 Hong Kong Cultural Centre	Gerard Salonga	Anthony Lun and friends Guests: Leung Chiu Fung Elisa Chan Kay Tse
Lio Kuokman × Johnny Yim I Journey of Time	2022 Hong Kong Cultural Centre	Lio Kuokman	Gigi Yim Windy Zhan Archie Sin

HK Phil × Ivana Wong 'The Missing Something' Concert	2023 Hong Kong City Hall	Joshua Tan	Ivana Wong
China Life (Overseas) Proudly Sponsors: HK Phil 50 – Symphonic Reunion	2024 Hong Kong Coliseum	Lio Kuokman	Elisa Chan Jay Fung Sandy Lam Anthony Lun Oscar Tao Cloud Wan Frances Yip

40 *Genius at Work*

Many soloists, conductors, composers, and other artists have worked with the orchestra. While countless names will be reluctantly missed in this chapter, my intention is to highlight the significance of some collaborations.

A Star-studded Opening

There was a dream cast at the opening of the Hong Kong Cultural Centre in 1989. Renowned artists, including sopranos Joan Sutherland and Jessye Norman, guitarist John Williams, conductors Richard Bonynge and David Willcocks, and the Bach Choir from the United Kingdom, took to the stage. HK Phil had the good fortune to work with them. When Joan Sutherland sang the challenging 'mad scene' from Donizetti's *Lucia di Lammermoor*, one found it difficult to believe that the diva was already 73. When Jessye Norman gave an encore of *Amazing Grace* (unaccompanied), everyone in the audience and players on stage were mesmerised while listening to that heavenly voice.

The Pleasure Is Ours

Players treasure opportunities to work with distinguished artists. Co-Principal Trumpet Christopher Moyse first started in 2005. The first performance he gave as a member of the orchestra was *Elektra* with Susan Bullock in the title role and the great Dame Gwyneth Jones as Klytaemnestra. He was in awe. That feeling returned a couple of months later as he shared the stage with Luciano Pavarotti. Chris recalls, 'It turned out to be the celebrated tenor's last performance in Hong Kong. He had to be seated during the performance, but that golden voice was still there!'

Audience Favourites

Such performers as Kiri Te Kanawa, Yo-Yo Ma, Joshua Bell, Yundi Li, Lang Lang, Yuja Wang and Ray Chen have proved to be audience favourites. It is sensational every time they work with HK Phil.

Violinist Joshua Bell's programmes are quite varied. With the HK Phil, on top of the well-known repertoire such as the Brahms, Tchaikovsky or Sibelius concertos, he also played Bernstein's 'Serenade' (after Plato's *Symposium*), John Corigliano's *The Red Violin*, and *The Elements*, a work co-written by five contemporary American composers. Tickets for all these programmes sold like hot cakes!

Lang Lang

Photo 40.1: Poster of Lang Lang's Symphony of Youth concert.

When Lang Lang first played with the orchestra on 12 and 13 February 1999, ticket sales were not as crazy as for his subsequent HK Phil collaborations. Yet the pair of concerts carries a special meaning. Lang Lang was only 16, and 'youth' was appropriately the main theme. He was joined by members of the Hong Kong Youth Symphony Orchestra, who played side-by-side with HK Phil's players. The performances did not take place in a concert hall but at Queen Elizabeth Stadium. Lang Lang chose to play Prokofiev's Third

Piano Concerto, a piece charged with youthful vitality. Other works in the programme, including Tchaikovsky's *Capriccio Italien* and the *1812 Overture*, were also full of energy. This programme, entitled Symphony of Youth, became the prelude to Lang Lang's many thrilling Hong Kong appearances to come.

A Timely Blessing

The orchestra was faced with a budget deficit in 1983. Luckily, a timely blessing came in December, when pop music icons Michael Kwan, Liza Wang, Danny Chan, Frances Yip, and Johnny Yip joined other performers to give four concerts at the Hong Kong Coliseum. It was HK Phil's first appearance at this grand venue. Over 40,000 tickets to this Music Extravaganza were sold, and the deficit was thankfully covered.

Photo 40.2: On top of popular singers, Music Extravaganza also provided a performance platform for two young and gifted musicians to display their talents. Sunny Wong (left) played the *erhu* and Warren Lee played the piano.

Double Delights from Perlman

There was another budget deficit in 1976. On 25 June, Itzhak Perlman took a trip to Hong Kong to make his HK Phil debut. That was a fund-raising concert conducted by Helen Quach. Ticket prices were higher than normal. Despite the overwhelming response (1,445 tickets sold), the total proceeds of HK$40,080 only slightly alleviated the orchestra's financial situation. That encounter with Perlman was especially meaningful, though. First, while Perlman was already a world-renowned violin virtuoso, his stage-partner was a 'young' orchestra that had turned professional just two years ago. Second, it was a double delight of two concertos (Mendelssohn and Tchaikovsky) in one concert. Itzhak Perlman has returned to Hong Kong many times, but just for recitals. The concert in 1976 remains the only time he performed here as a concerto soloist.

So Hau-leung was instrumental in bringing Perlman to Hong Kong. The orchestra could not afford the violin virtuoso's fee. However, having learned that Perlman was fond of Chinese cuisine, the general manager asked if he would like to accept a modest fee and come enjoy the glorious Chinese food as a bonus. Apparently, that proposal was mouth-watering to Perlman.

So Hau-leung was deeply impressed by Perlman's sense of humour and humility. When they met at the airport, Perlman began their conversation with a question, 'Which concerto am I going to play?'

Photo 40.3: Itzhak Perlman with conductor Helen Quach.

Dr P. P. Chiu, a loyal supporter of HK Phil, kindly invited Perlman to stay at his place in Repulse Bay. Only upon arrival did the management discover that the elegant room was on the second floor. Perlman did not show any sign of displeasure and smilingly made his way up the stairway on his crutches.

Twists and Turns

In December 1982, Vladimir Ashkenazy made his HK Phil debut in Brahms's Piano Concerto no. 1 for a fundraising concert. The concert was directed by the orchestra's concertmaster and assistant conductor Carl Pini. Everything went smoothly. In February 1983, the orchestra announced plans to invite the multi-talented entertainer Danny Kaye to appear in a fundraising concert in April. Kaye did not read music, but one of his fortes was conducting. In fact, NY Phil was among the list of notable orchestras which has performed under his baton. Unfortunately, Kaye had an emergency operation, and the concert was put forward to February the following year. All tickets were already gone for this postponed performance. However, the orchestra was informed that Kaye was sick again. It seemed unlikely that a replacement of that calibre could be engaged at such short notice. However, luck was on HK Phil's side. The famous British lyricist and writer Tim Rice would join Elaine Paige and Colm Wilkinson, two legendary singers famous for their performances in *Cats* and *Les Misérables* respectively, to give the fundraiser in Hong Kong.

It was Tim Rice's first time singing with an orchestra in public. After the concert, he sent an amusing telex to Cynthia Hydes, the orchestra's PR manager:

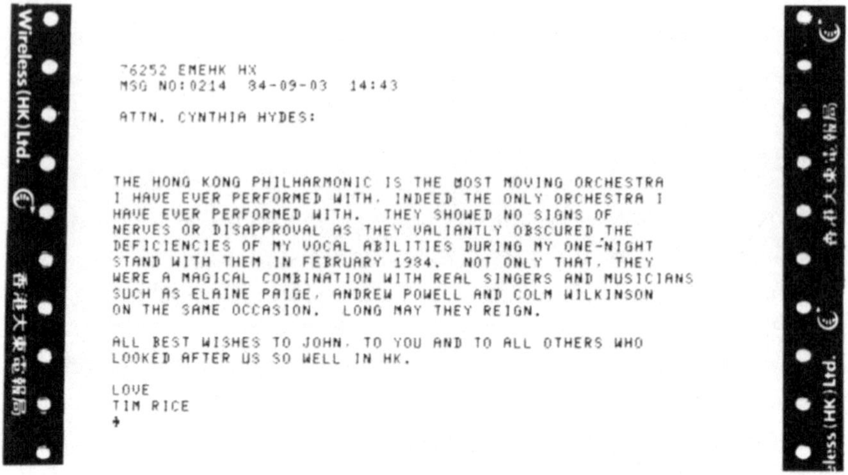

76252 EMEHK HX
MSG NO:0214 84-09-03 14:43

ATTN. CYNTHIA HYDES:

THE HONG KONG PHILHARMONIC IS THE MOST MOVING ORCHESTRA I HAVE EVER PERFORMED WITH. INDEED THE ONLY ORCHESTRA I HAVE EVER PERFORMED WITH. THEY SHOWED NO SIGNS OF NERVES OR DISAPPROVAL AS THEY VALIANTLY OBSCURED THE DEFICIENCIES OF MY VOCAL ABILITIES DURING MY ONE-NIGHT STAND WITH THEM IN FEBRUARY 1984. NOT ONLY THAT. THEY WERE A MAGICAL COMBINATION WITH REAL SINGERS AND MUSICIANS SUCH AS ELAINE PAIGE, ANDREW POWELL AND COLM WILKINSON ON THE SAME OCCASION. LONG MAY THEY REIGN.

ALL BEST WISHES TO JOHN. TO YOU AND TO ALL OTHERS WHO LOOKED AFTER US SO WELL IN HK.

LOVE
TIM RICE
+

Photo 40.4: A telex from Tim Rice to the HK Phil.

Photo 40.5: Tim Rice.

Photo 40.6: Elaine Paige.

Farewell Symphonies

Although some top-notch artists who worked with the orchestra have already passed away, their glorious performances remain unforgettable to veteran concertgoers.

Distinguished Chinese baritone Yi-Kwei Sze made a name for himself with appearances at major concert halls and opera houses around the world. His recording of Zhao Yuanren's 'How Can I Forget Him?' is a classic rendition of the famous Chinese art song. On 19 October 1979, he appeared on stage with the orchestra as part of the Asian Arts Festival. One of the songs he sang was Alexander Tchnerpnin's 'Of Things Light and Earnest'. During his lifetime, Tchnerpnin was closely connected with China. Yi-Kwei Sze was a friend of the composer. That performance was particularly memorable.

The teacher of Cuban pianist Jorge Bolet was Franz Liszt's student. In 1960, Liszt's biographical movie *Song Without End* won the Academy Award for Best Music Score. The piano part was played by Bolet. His admiration of Liszt was apparent at the HK Phil concerts on 18 and 19 March 1987 – it was Liszt's transcription of Franz Schubert's *Wanderer Fantasy*. The year after, Bolet's health began to deteriorate, and he died in 1990.

Anyone who has watched the documentary film *From Mao to Mozart* finds maestro Isaac Stern unforgettable. The violinist and humanitarian appeared on Hong Kong's performance podiums on many occasions. In fact, he was a testament of the development of classical music in Hong Kong, having given recitals at Empire Theatre, City Hall, and the Cultural Centre. His only concerto performance with HK Phil took place on 1 December 1997. He was already 77 then, but the audience was treated to two concertos – Mozart's Fifth and Max Bruch's First. The maestro made an interesting remark. He said that the combined duration of the two concertos was shorter than a solo recital!

Along with top-ranking orchestras such as the Cleveland Orchestra, NY Phil, and Philharmonia, Lorin Maazel appeared in Hong Kong frequently. The only time that he came to conduct the HK Phil was another double delight.

Photo 40.7: The Legend Continues – poster of Isaac Stern's only collaboration with HK Phil.

On 1 and 2 November 2013, he first conducted *The Ring Without Words* – his arrangement of Wagner's *Ring* cycle. Concertmaster Jing Wang has vivid memories of the maestro: 'He knew his *Ring Without Words* inside out. During rehearsal, he closed his eyes and leaned against the conductor podium's railing for a long time, while the strings were repeating a figure for like sixty-nine bars. I thought he was sleeping. However, at the seventieth bar when we finished repeating, he opened his eyes and made an important cue. It was spot on!'

On 7 November, it was the second Hong Kong performance of Britten's *War Requiem* (2013 was the hundredth anniversary of the birth of the British composer). After these two programmes, Maazel was to return to conduct the orchestra in the complete Brahms symphonies in November 2014. Unfortunately, he passed away in July of that year. The concert series was conducted by Perry So instead.

Many other artists have left a legacy on HK Phil's performance platforms. The following are a few memorable moments.

Photo 40.8: Shen Rong.

Shen Rong

Recordings of the *Butterfly Lovers' Concerto* were released in the 1960s. The versions featuring Yu Lina and Shen Rong were the most popular. At the Shanghai Conservatory, the two ladies were fellow students of the work's composers He Zhanhao and Chen Gang. Shen Rong moved to Hong Kong in the 1980s. From 1986 to 2008 she was second violinist at HK Phil, serving the orchestra for almost a quarter of a century. In June 1988, Shen Rong appeared at the Hong Kong Coliseum as soloist in the *Butterfly Lovers' Concerto*, one of the most authentic live performances of the work.

Monique Duphil

The late Jay Humeston was HK Phil's principal cello. Hong Kong also had the good fortune to welcome Monique Duphil, his pianist wife. Monique had a remarkable solo career, including seven performances with Eugene Ormandy and the Philadelphia Orchestra. I have done a rough calculation: from 1979 to 1986, Monique was featured in at least fifteen pieces with the orchestra (not counting the innumerable chamber performances she gave with HK Phil members). Among the works she performed with HK Phil were concertos by Mozart, Chopin, Ravel, Rachmaninov (including the lesser-known no. 1, conducted by Mommer in 1979), and Bartók's *Concerto for Two Pianos, Percussion and Orchestra*. In 1985, she was soloist in Bernstein's Symphony no. 2, 'Age of Anxiety' (the composer was then still alive). On top of that, she also played the harpsichord in Bach's Brandenburg Concerto no. 5, and thus her repertoire with HK Phil spread from Baroque to the twentieth century. She may perhaps be the soloist who has played the most piano concertos with the orchestra.

Photo 40.9: Monique Duphil.

Myung-Whun Chung's First Mahler Fourth

In October 1982, Myung-Whun Chung first conducted HK Phil. He brought with him two programmes. At that time, he was known to the world chiefly as a Tchaikovsky Piano Competition winner. He was still in the beginning stages of his conducting

Photo 40.10: Myung-Whun Chung.

career and did not yet have his own orchestra. In HK Phil's tenth anniversary publication, *Celebration*, he wrote, 'To the members of the Hong Kong Philharmonic and Cynthia (Hydes): thanks for a wonderful two weeks and for my first Mahler 4th.' Today he is a sought-after conductor, and Mahler is still close to his heart.

Photo 40.11: Maxim Shostakovich.

Shostakovich × 3

In 1981, Maxim Shostakovich, son of the great Soviet composer, defected from the USSR with his son. In January 1982, they gave a performance of Shostakovich's Piano Concerto no. 2 with HK Phil. The piece was written for Maxim in 1957. Twenty-five years later, the soloist was Maxim's son Dmitri (same name as the grandfather). In the same year, Maxim accepted the invitation to be

Photo 40.12: Maxim's son Dmitri Shostakovich.

HK Phil's principal guest conductor, a post he held until 1985. During his term, many astounding performances were given.

Prince Charles's Birthday Song

British composer Michael Tippett shared the stage with the orchestra on 21 and 22 January 1984. As conductor and composer, he brought the Suite in D to Hong Kong. It was a piece written for the birth of Prince Charles. Today, the Prince has become the King. In fact, thirty-nine years after the work was played by HK Phil, the same piece was heard again at the King's coronation.

Other composers who conducted their own works include Krzysztof Penderecki, Bright Sheng, Tan Dun, and of course, Joe Hisaishi!

The above are in past tense. Let's end in future tense. I have asked some die-hard classical music fans the same question: 'Which artists would you like to see making their debuts with HK Phil?' Here are some names:

Daniel Barenboim (conductor)

Herbert Blomstedt (conductor)

Riccardo Chailly (conductor)

Christoph Poppen (conductor)

Kirill Petrenko (conductor)

Martha Argerich (pianist)

Mitsuko Uchida (pianist)

Krystian Zimerman (pianist)

Angela Gheorghiu (soprano)

Natalie Dessay (soprano)

Cecilia Bartoli (mezzo-soprano)

Elīna Garanča (mezzo-soprano)

Janine Jansen (violinist and violist)

Photo 40.13: 'Get ready ladies!' Some artists like Ray Chen are sensations at backstage too. Courtesy of Zhang Xi.

Julia Fischer (violinist and pianist) – would be nice if she can play two concertos, each featuring one instrument!

Do you have any other names in mind?[1]

[1] When the Chinese version of this book was published, the tenor Jonas Kaufmann's name was on the list. He did make his Hong Kong début with the orchestra in February 2025. Unfortunately, he was sick and the first concert had to be cancelled. The second show went on as scheduled. Despite the problems with his voice, Kaufmann captured everyone's heart with remarkable artistry and utmost sincerity. The majority of audience members were on their feet at curtain calls. Under the baton of Jochen Rieder, the orchestra played with restrained power without trading off the intensity of the music. The evening was a true display of everyone's professionalism.

41 *The Doppleganger*

It was talk of the town when famous film music composer Joe Hisaishi came to Hong Kong in May 2018.

A few days before the show, Stage Manager Steven Chan was walking through the Cultural Centre foyer. Suddenly, a sincere music-lover asked to have a selfie with him. It was then that Steven realised his face, height, and hair style all bore resemblance to those of the maestro.

Having learned about this delightful episode, a colleague in the office gave Steven a nickname which is hard to put into English. I will try anyway. The first word '久' in Hisaishi's name (久石譲) sounds exactly like 'nine' in Cantonese. Steven's new alias was '十 ("ten") 石譲'! The time came when the genuine Hisaishi met Steven for the first time at rehearsal. The two had a great laugh and took lovely pictures.

Finally, the concert was going to begin. Some audience members found it strange that the conductor was not backstage preparing to perform; instead, he was tidying up music stands and chairs on stage!

Photo 41.1: The Doppelganger!

Photo 41.2: Steven Chan receiving the Lifetime Achievement Award by the League of China Orchestras in 2019.

Steven Chan is highly accomplished in his profession too. He joined HK Phil in 1977 (he actually played the trumpet as a freelancer previously) and served the orchestra until his retirement in 2020. In 2019, he was bestowed with a Lifetime Achievement Award by the League of China Orchestras for his outstanding service as the orchestra's stage manager.

HK Phil's Former Executive Director Vennie Ho was a longtime colleague of Steven. She told me a little anecdote. Steven never took leave. He even wanted to stay at work the night his son got married! The management eventually insisted that on the 'big day', he should be at the banquet instead. He 'relented', but the story continued.

Vennie remarked that, at the concert, while the stage manager was away to perform his other 'duty' as father-in-law, the stage was set, ready for a cello concerto performance. Yet, the cello stool was missing! Guess who the soloist was?

Yo-Yo Ma . . .

42 *Yo-Yo Ma*

Yo-Yo Ma's Hong Kong performances have almost always been full houses. I say 'almost always' because his Hong Kong debut recital on 24 March 1977 at City Hall Concert Hall, when he was just 21 years old, had a show-up rate of less than 45%. Forty-four years later, for his recital on 6 November 2023, a real-name ticketing system had to be adopted and it was over-subscribed by 500%! A few thousand music-lovers, including me, were disappointed!

The master cellist is a real sensation. His concerto performance with HK Phil two days later was a full house: in fact, all tickets were gone shortly after ticket sales began.

As the stage door on the left opened, the audience was immediately captivated by a gentle and familiar smile, which brought a ray of sunshine into the concert hall. The audience responded with cheers and thundering applause. Utmost excitement was in the air! Not a note had been played yet, but Yo-Yo Ma had already won everyone's heart with his charisma.

The soloist does not have to play the first four minutes of the Dvořák concerto. However, Yo-Yo was enjoying every moment. When the violins, clarinet or horn had their shares of melodies, Yo-Yo smiled and turned his body slightly towards the respective musicians to show his appreciation. Who would not feel respected by such a gesture?

During rehearsals, many players took pictures with Yo-Yo, and he graciously entertained all their requests. The cello section was over the moon when they had a chance to take a group photo with him.

Photo 42.1: Yo-Yo Ma and HK Phil's cellists.

First Associate Concertmaster Leung Kin-fung posted a little story on social media. He failed to obtain a ticket for his wife, who decided to go back to her childhood home in Taiwan!! When Yo-Yo heard about this, he recorded a video clip at backstage specifically for Mrs Leung. How sweet!

Although he had played the concerto countless times, he delivered, as always, a refreshing performance to the Hong Kong audience. It is rare to see a soloist play with so much eye-contact and joy. This is his unique way of communicating with the conductor and players. Concertmaster Jing Wang made this remark, 'There is an enchanting feeling sitting next to him. He knows his solo part too well. It was like he was saying to himself, "I'm going to focus on something else"; and his solo seemed secondary to the communication and musical conversations that was happening between him and all the various voices.'

The house was brought down, and Yo-Yo was as sincere as ever when returning onto the stage to acknowledge the ravished audience's roaring ovation.

Another climax of the evening was a special encore, which was preceded by Yo-Yo's words of wisdom.

He said that when Dvořák was director of the National Conservatory of Music of America, a student named Harry Burleigh sang African-American spirituals for him. Had Dvořák not encountered this genre of music, the 'New World' Symphony, 'American' Quartet, and the cello concerto which the audience had just listened to would not have existed. Yo-Yo then played an encore, which was a mix of the spiritual *Nobody Knows the Trouble I've Seen* and the theme from the second movement of the 'New World' Symphony.

Yo-Yo is more than a distinguished musician. His intelligence was revealed in his choice of an encore, which tells a story. While adding an extra flavour to the piece, he was making it a more remarkable experience for audience members.

Yo-Yo has always been a great communicator. During his last visit to the territory, he chatted with 200 students and staff members at The Chinese University of Hong Kong. In 1986, the privilege was given to members of the Friends of the Philharmonic, who also attended his first rehearsal with the orchestra.

Photo 42.2: Yo-Yo Ma in conversation with Friends of the Philharmonic in 1986.

43 *Masters from Early Years*

Resources were scarce in the 1950s and 1960s. International travel was much less popular than today. Yet, as amateur groups, SBO and the pre-professional HK Phil were able to work with professional musicians from abroad. There were quite a few notable names too.

Warsaw Concerto

For the great 1940s movie *Dangerous Moonlight*, British composer Richard Addinsell wrote the *Warsaw Concerto* – a highly successful piece in the style of Rachmaninov. The piano part was played by Louis Kentner, friend of his Hungarian compatriots Béla Bartók and Zoltán Kodály. On 28 April 1953, he played Beethoven's Piano Concerto no. 3 with SBO at Queen's College and became the first musician of that international reputation to work with the orchestra.

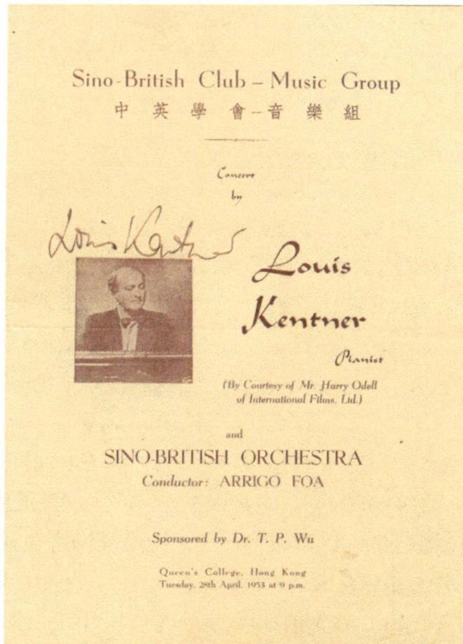

Sino-British Club – Music Group
中英學會－音樂組
Concert by
Louis Kentner
Pianist
(By Courtesy of Mr. Harry Odell of International Films, Ltd.)
and
SINO-BRITISH ORCHESTRA
Conductor: ARRIGO FOA
Sponsored by Dr. T. P. Wu
Queen's College, Hong Kong
Tuesday, 28th April, 1953 at 9 p.m.

Photo 43.1: Doming Lam's collection. The late composer was a violinist at SBO. Courtesy of Kathy Lam.

Another master was the Polish-born pianist Jan Smeterlin. He was a student of the great piano virtuoso Leopold Godowsky, and friend of the renowned Polish composer Karol Szymanowski. Smeterlin, a great interpreter of Chopin's music, brought to the Hong Kong audience Chopin's first piano concerto on 23 July 1954.

Virtuoso violinist Ruggiero Ricci has shared the stage with SBO and HK Phil on many occasions. His first visit took place on 21 June 1957. Along with SBO, he played the Beethoven concerto. On 5 and 6 October 1984, when HK Phil celebrated their tenth anniversary as a professional body, Ricci delightfully chose to play the same piece!

Photo 43.2: Ruggiero Ricci.

Julius Katchen

Pianist Julius Katchen performed in Hong Kong twice. The first time was in a recital in 1955. The second was on 31 July 1957. The first half was solo works: Franck's *Prelude, Chorale and Fugue*, and Schubert's *Wanderer's Fantasy*. The second half was Beethoven's 'Emperor' Concerto, with SBO conducted by Arrigo Foa. That became the last SBO concert that featured an acclaimed international artist, because its operations were basically taken over by HK Phil. The latter was inaugurated in August of the same year.

Photo 43.3: Julius Katchen

In addition to the visiting artists mentioned above, in the 1950s and earlier, various musicians from overseas chose to settle in Hong Kong. Here are four of them who made significant contributions to the local music scene.

Doctor, Musician, and Archaeologist

Born in Siberia in 1916, Solomon Bard grew up in Harbin, prepared for his matriculation exam in Shanghai, studied medicine at HKU, became a prisoner of war in the Sham Shui Po camp, was repatriated to the United Kingdom after World War II, and returned to Hong Kong to pursue his medical career. Music occupied a special position in all phases of his fascinating life. Even in captivity during the war, he founded and conducted an 'orchestra' and gave performances behind barbed wire. As a boy, his education had included a few years of intensive training at a music school. He played a variety of instruments including piano, violin, and flute. With such a distinctive and resourceful background, no wonder Bard was asked to be the first formal conductor of SBO, leading its first concert in April 1948.

Bard relinquished the baton to Arrigo Foa in 1953 and remained a player (including the oboe when the position needed to be filled), deputy conductor, concertmaster, SBO's committee member, unofficial doctor and sometimes even driver! He remained wholeheartedly involved with the pre-professional HK Phil while pursuing his medical profession at Hong Kong University. For years, Bard was a key figure in the operation of these performing bodies. As quoted by Oliver Chou in the HK Phil's fortieth anniversary book, in 1973, Dr Bard announced the orchestra's change of status at a press conference, 'The time has come to make a determined effort to upgrade it into a competent professional orchestra worthy of support.' He was then Hong Kong Philharmonic Society's chairman. His vision has clearly come true.

Further pages were turned in Bard's remarkable life. After retiring from medical practice in 1976, his next calling was to be an archaeologist. Musically, he was involved with the Hong Kong Chinese Orchestra in the 1980s. At times, he was the orchestra's full-time conductor and assistant music director.

In 1993, he moved to Australia, where he passed away in 2014 at the age of ninety-eight. Bard was a true legend.

Photo 43.4: Solomon Bard.

A Conductor from Shanghai

In 1921, Mario Paci,[1] conductor of the Shanghai Public Band (predecessor of the Shanghai Municipal Council Symphony Orchestra and the Shanghai Symphony Orchestra), left for Italy to look for new players. He met violinist Arrigo Foa, who was a recent graduate of Milan Conservatory, his alma mater. Upon Paci's invitation, Foa joined him in Shanghai to become the Shanghai orchestra's concertmaster, and subsequently assumed the post of associate conductor. In 1937, Foa became conductor in chief. He came to Hong Kong in 1952. The following year, Solomon Bard, who was SBO's conductor, passed on the baton to him. He remained in the position until 1969, directing countless performances given by SBO and the pre-professional HK Phil. He was a well-known violinist and recording artist when he was in Shanghai.

[1] He was also a distinguished pianist and educator. Some early-generation Chinese pianists including Fou Ts'ong, Zhou Guangren and Wu Yili were his students.

His forte was in chamber music. He also taught many students, one of whom was the composer Doming Lam, an active member of SBO. Another one was Y. S. Liu, who has played at the pre-professional HK Phil for years. Foa died in 1981, and is buried at the Jewish Cemetery in Happy Valley.

Photo 43.5: Arrigo Foa and SBO.

Classmate of Prokofiev

The programme of SBO's concert on 10 and 15 December 1953 writes: 'The SBO has much pleasure in presenting in these concerts the first performances of this Piano Concertino by Harry Ore, with the composer himself as the soloist.'

Harry Ore, whose native country is Latvia, received his music education at the St. Petersburg Conservatory. He was a pupil of Liadov and among his classmates were Prokofiev and Miaskovsky.

He came to Hong Kong in 1921. Apart from short visits to other Asian cities, he basically made Hong Kong his home. On top of being an accomplished pianist, he was a piano teacher and composer. He frequently collaborated with SBO, including in a rendition of his own work – *Latvian Concerto*.

In the aforementioned concerts, his multiple talents were demonstrated. In Mozart's Concerto for Two Pianos, K. 365, he was joined by his student Linda Hu. The two cadenzas appearing in the work's first and third movements were written by him. In the second half, Ore played his own work – *Concertino for the Young*. One can tell by the title of the piece that the pianist/composer had a heart for music education. He was deeply interested in Chinese culture too. Some of his piano arrangements of Chinese traditional music such as *Liu Yao Jin* and *Rain Falling on Bamboo Leaves* have been published.

Photo 43.6: Harry Ore. Courtesy of Oliver Chou.

Cortot's Student

Annarosa Taddei was a student of Alfredo Casella and Alfred Cortot. Cortot was in fact one of the official witnesses at Taddei's wedding. On 24 and 26 October 1956, she played Mendelssohn's Piano Concerto no. 1 with SBO. In the house programme, Cortot's words were quoted: 'I learn that my remarkable disciple Miss Annarosa Taddei is going to the Far East on a concert tour. I do not know how to stress the pianistic and musical virtues of this truly great artist, who has just toured

Europe and the United States with such justifiable success.' Her tour also resulted in a romantic story: she met Dr Eric Vio (who once took the helm at Canossa Hospital) in Hong Kong and subsequently got married. While in Hong Kong, she played with the orchestra on various occasions including Beethoven's fourth concerto on 25 February 1959 at Loke Yew Hall, Hong Kong University. Taddei taught piano too. So Hau-leung, the first general manager of the professional HK Phil, was her student. (So Hau-leung also learned from Harry Ore.)

After spending years in Hong Kong, Taddei went back to Italy. She returned to Hong Kong occasionally to perform and adjudicate. Her commitment to music education was realised in Italy: a foundation was set up in her name in 2012 to organise international competitions and award scholarships to aspiring young winners.

During HK Phil's pre-professional days, other overseas artists collaborated with the orchestra. The list includes Australian violinist Beryl Kimber (who was David Oistrakh's student), American pianist Ann Shein, French flautist Jean-Pierre Rampal, Hungarian pianist Andor Földes (who was Bartók student), and the Australian horn player Barry Tuckwell.

A Commissioned Work by an Oscar Laureate

This one was really special . . .

On 8 December 1968, HK Phil celebrated its twenty-first anniversary,[2] and a commissioned work was written by Malcolm Arnold. Under the direction of Arrigo Foa, *Hong Kong Anniversary Overture* was given its world premiere. In the house programme, words from the British composer were quoted: 'When the work is published it will be called *Hong Kong Anniversary Overture*. This is what it is, and it helps to explain the flavour of the music which I hope is not only joyous, but is definitely celebrating a birthday in Hong Kong.'

[2] Counting from SBO's inauguration in 1947.

Arnold won an Academy Award for his scoring for the movie *The Bridge on the River Kwai* in 1958. He was probably the first Oscar winner to have written a work for HK Phil.

The 1970s

Hong Kong's economy took off in the 1970s. Compared with early years, HK Phil clearly had more resources to deploy. This was apparent with a remarkable list of soloists appearing in the first season's subscription brochure. However, for various reasons, some of them did not make it to Hong Kong. Those who did appear included Christian Edinger who made debut with Berlin Philharmonic at the age of nineteen, Rudolf Buchbinder, winner of the Van Cliburn Piano Competition, and Hong Kong favourite Takako Nishizaki.

An interesting fact: at the 2023/24 season, it had been fifty years since Buchbinder's first visit. Half a century ago, he played one work – Schumann's concerto; and this time there were two: Beethoven's Fourth and Fifth.

A passion for music may be a reason for longevity!

Photo 43.7: Jaap van Zweden shaking hands with Rudolf Buchbinder in September 2023.

44 *The Joy of Sharing*

Music, when shared, can bring happiness.

Let us travel back to school concerts in the 1980s–1990s.

A school welcomed the HK Phil Brass Quintet, who captured the attention of students with their shiny instruments.

Trumpet player Brian Thomson played a famous tune which was often heard in a TV commercial for gastric medicine. Everyone responded with a big laugh!

Trombone player Allistar Gaskin took an object out from his bag. It looked like a cooking pot. A student was asked to come onto the stage to help. A girl, with full support from her fellow schoolmates, volunteered. Looking closer, that 'pot' was in fact rings of metal collapsed into a cylindrical shape. The tiny girl was instructed to hold tight to the outer part of that chubby object, while Allistar pulled the innermost ring. Slowly, a long conical tube of about two metres was formed. It was a Tibetan horn. Next, Allistar asked the girl to put one end of the instrument (the bell part) on her shoulder, while from two metres away, he played a note which was resonant and exotic. The girl looked uneasy while taking part in that 'performance'.

Tuba player Lee Tsarmaklis brought his enormous instrument to centre stage to show students how low the instrument could go. It was dead silent while everyone waited eagerly to hear those low notes. Lee started high and went down a major scale note by note. In the final octave, he made it slower and slower. As the notes went down, so did his body. He first bowed his head, then bent his knees, his back, knelt on one leg, and crouched, before lying flat on the floor to play the lowest note – a B flat. Roaring applause followed.

Down-to-Earth Performance

That was literally a down-to-earth performance. Music is an unspoken language. That musical and visual presentation, which everyone could understand, undoubtedly left a lasting impression on students and teachers. Musicians naturally find it rewarding when their pleasure in playing is shared with listeners.

Whenever he recalls these happy moments at schools, horn player Joe Kirtley is always thrilled:

> It was so much fun spending time with kids. There was a section in the *Happy Birthday Variations* where the tune was in minor mode. The rhythm was slow and dotted, making it sound like a funeral march! Brian did not have to play, but he always made it his show time! He would put his head into his hands, pretending to be sobbing. While some students started laughing, the four of us tried to hold it together, and played on, with some difficulty! One time, Brian was perhaps having a bit too much fun? He took out a handkerchief to blow his nose. It was impossible for us to continue. The piece ended in a mess of uncontrolled laughter both on stage and from the audience. The hall was filled with thunderous applause and cheers. Those kids were so lovely and sincere.

Sincere Players Too

Oboist Peter Cooper played the theme song of *Enjoy Yourself Tonight*, a popular TV show at the time,[1] before introducing other players with his fluent Cantonese. Kids simply loved this tall, goodlooking, and talented American. Next, flautist Philip Dikeman introduced everyone to the opening of Debussy's *Prélude à l'après-midi d'un faune*. The kids

[1] In recent years, 'Let It Go' from *Frozen* and themes from computer games *Super Mario Bros* and *Angry Birds* have become popular choices.

held their breath, mesmerised by the rounded and sonorous notes which magically filled every corner of the school hall.

Home-Made Horn

In the woodwind quintet's school visits, the only brass player was the French horn player. Homer Lee carried with him a huge shell and stood at the side of the stage. He asked if the audience would like to hear the sound of a shell. A big round of applause erupted. A moment later, he held a plastic tube attached to a funnel and a mouthpiece. With the kids curious about what this weird-looking thing was, Homer buzzed into the mouthpiece and a fanfare was heard! The audience was surprised to hear a majestic march played on that home-made 'instrument'.

For the non-stop rhythmic pattern in *Carmen*'s 'Habanera', players would invite a student to join them on the castanets. Whether it was a

Photo 44.1: Homer's home-made instrument.

volunteer, an unwilling guy who was pushed up on stage by classmates, or an embarrassed teacher, handling the rhythm was not a problem. He or she would always be enthusiastically cheered by students.

Photo 44.2: The rhythmic pattern in *Carmen*'s 'Habanera'.

The Shortest Clue

There was a quiz towards the latter part of the show. The emcee said, 'Players will soon play to you a short excerpt of the next piece. Whoever knows the answer will receive a HK Phil T-shirt! Listen carefully, the excerpt is really short!' The audience made no noise and eagerly waited for the passage to come. The quintet just played one single chord that lasted one second! While the audience felt amused, excited, and lost, there was always someone who came up with the right answer – Wedding March from *A Midsummer Night's Dream*! That A–E–F#–C chord has a signature character.

Players named the last work in the programme – *The Magic Hand* – and directed the audience's attention to Kam Shui, the bassoon player. The piece was lively, and very soon, the final note was played. Attached to the top of the bassoon, a plastic glove slowly inflated. Kam Shui waved his instrument, and it was as if that cute little 'hand' was waving goodbye to the boys and girls and their teachers too. The trick was a natural scientific phenomenon. A plastic glove was tied to the tip of the bassoon by a rubber band. When the lowest note of the bassoon is played, all holes on the instrument are covered. Hence, the pressure inside the tubes will inflate the glove.

In the early professional days, HK Phil did not have that many commitments. Sometimes, the whole orchestra would give concerts at schools. As the orchestra got busier, schools were visited by smaller brass, woodwind, percussion, and string ensembles.

Photo 44.3: A concert at a school in the orchestra's early professional days. The conductor in the picture is the multi-talented David Gwilt. Courtesy of David Gwilt.

Photo 44.4: HK Phil performed at SKH Bishop Mok Sau Tseng Secondary School in Tai Po in 1981.

Shall We Dance?

Apart from ensemble visits, HK Phil also put on one-hour performances at proper concert venues and invited schools to send students and teachers to take part. One time, First Associate Concertmaster Leung Kin-fung invited Pan Lingjuan, Hong Kong Dance Company's principal dancer, to curate a programme which was essentially a 'dance through the ages', covering baroque to modern dances. She demonstrated a number of dance moves accompanied by beautiful music played by the orchestra. It was an eye-opener to the audience, who ended up understanding more about how music and body movements correlate. Kin-fung was the concertmaster as well as emcee. At one point, he partnered with Lingjuan to demonstrate a *pas de deux*. Next, he invited students to come on stage and learn how to dance with the orchestra. The boys and girls started getting excited. The invitation was further extended to teachers! The whole house went wild as students eagerly nominated their class teachers to give it a go. To dance in public is not most Hongkongers' cup of tea!

At these joyful adventures, students and teachers are exposed to a wealth of lovely music. They pick up knowledge and fun facts and realise that classical music is indeed quite pleasing to the ear. As for players, they also have a good time. Although all of them are masters of their instruments, at the same time they are very approachable.

Promoting music and building new audiences have always been delightful experiences.

Photo 44.5: On 27 March 2010, HK Phil visited Shap Pat Heung Rural Committee Kung Yik She Primary School to give two community concerts. Perry So, who was Associate Conductor then, led a group of students from Q.E.S. Old Students' Association Branch Primary School to perform Stravinsky's *The Firebird*. These young dancers rehearsed for more than a month before taking to the stage.

Photo 44.6 and Photo 44.7: Transportation Officer So Kan Pong was a HK Phil veteran. In 2012, he drove the orchestra's truck to Tuen Mun for the Music for Smart Kids concert promotion. Colleagues from the marketing department distributed leaflets and souvenirs to Tuen Mun residents.

Photo 44.8 and Photo 44.9: As part of the orchestra's fiftieth anniversary celebration, the Rhythm of the City community performances took place at various cultural landmarks and shopping malls, bringing music into the community. In Music Journey with Star Ferry, HK Phil's recordings of works by different composers, all inspired by the theme of the sea, were played on board.

45 *Our Own Opuses*

How 'Hong Kong' is HK Phil's repertoire?

In SBO's years (1947–1957), works from the Classical and Romantic periods were the orchestra's core repertoire. There were some Baroque and choral works too. This mix reflects the size of the orchestra, the conductors' tastes, and the audience's preferences. Contemporary works seldom appeared; an exception was the *Pastoral Suite* by Lars-Erik Larsson (born 1908), which was played on 24 and 26 November 1956. As for works written by Hong Kong-based composers, the two Harry Ore concertos mentioned in chapter 43, 'Masters from Early Years' were real rarities.

Photo 45.1: Composer Doming Lam at the 2012 Swire Symphony Under the Stars. Thousands of music-lovers joined him to listen to his arrangement of *Caprice on Flowery Spring River*.

Seventy-Year Partnership

Doming was a violinist in SBO during the orchestra's early years. Driven by a fervent interest in music composition, he subsequently went to study in Canada and the United States. When he returned in 1965, the amateur HK Phil put on a concert entirely of his works. Over the years, the orchestra showcased his compositions on numerous occasions. Doming appeared on HK Phil's concert platform for the last time in October 2020. In that concert, his *Thanksgiving to Joe-Kwan, the Kitchen God* was part of the programme. The orchestra even arranged a lion dance, which perfectly matched the festive mood of the piece. The 94-year-old composer was in a wheelchair when he came onto the stage to acknowledge the applause from the audience.

In the 1960s and 1970s, the orchestra also showcased works by other innovative composers, including Wong Yok-yee's Symphony no. 1 and Prelude from *Festival of Hong Kong* Suite,[1] and Lin Sheng-shih's *Tibetan Sketches* and *In Memoriam*.

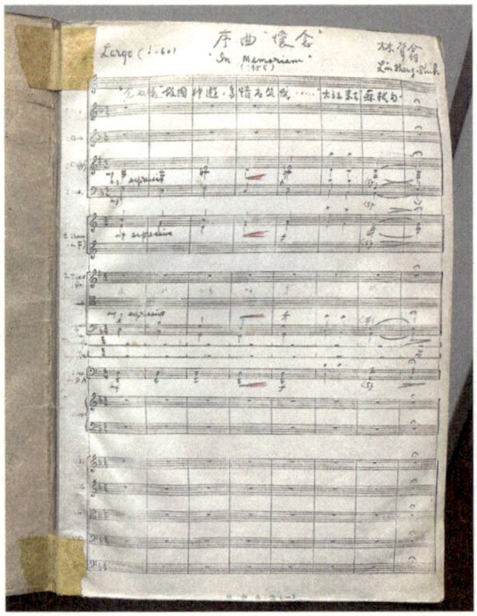

Photo 45.2: First page of the manuscripts of Lin Sheng-shih's *In Memoriam*, written in 1955. Courtesy of Winnie Lin.

1 It was a set of four pieces premiered at the first Festival of Hong Kong in 1969. The other three were Chen Chien-hua's *Sunrise*, Lin Sheng-shih's *Edinburgh Place*, and Doming Lam's *Tai-Ping Shan Panorama*. The concert's programme provided background information about the work: 'This "Festival Suite" which was commissioned by Radio Hong Kong for the Festival of Hong Kong, consists of separate movements by four of Hong Kong's leading composers. The idea behind such a commission has been to produce a piece of music suitable for the festive occasion and at the same time to encourage our local composers. A certain disparity of style is inevitable in a work written jointly by four composers, but there has been an attempt to give unity to the suite by the use of a five-note motif. This motif (Ray–Doh–La–Mi–Soh) was selected at random and appears in different forms in each of the four sections.'

Chances were still limited. As time went by, the situation evolved. In the 1980s, Daniel Law's *Ode from the Nestorian Monument* was programmed three times in the 1980/81 season. The composer reflected recently, 'I feel that a work performed three times by one orchestra is good, and I laud the effort of HK Phil's willingness to perform new works of local composers. It must be very encouraging for young composers.'

The orchestra also started getting involved in large-scale events for the promotion of new music: the Contemporary Chinese Composers Festival; Musicarama; Asian Arts Festival; A Celebration of Hong Kong Artists – City Hall Silver Jubilee; and all three times (1988, 2002, and 2007) when the International Society for Contemporary Music took the stage in Hong Kong. Audiences got the chance to hear HK Phil in performances of works written by local composers.

HK Phil began to take a more active role in commissioning Hong Kong composers to write new works too. Chan Wing Wah, for instance, marked HK Phil's tenth and twentieth professional seasons with *Celebration* (1984) and *Elevation* (1994) respectively. Some longer pieces by the composer were commissioned and premiered by the orchestra too. In the 1990s, he and Victor Chan became HK Phil's Composers-in-Residence.

David Atherton is a champion of new music. Shortly after he became music director, he invited many local composers to each write a short concert-opener.

Over the years, the orchestra has worked with numerous Hong Kong composers, among them Law Wing-fai, Joshua Chan, and Richard Tsang. With *Dragon Signs*, Richard Tsang was awarded CASH's (Composers and Authors Society of Hong Kong) Golden Sail Music Award (Best Serious Composition) in 2002.

Local works have not only been played locally. For instance, John Chen's *Dragon Wings* has been played seven times in Europe and Korea. Chan Kai-young's *Spiraling Dreamscape* received its world premiere in Shanghai in 2019. In the 2013/14 season, Fung Lam, who was then composer-in-residence, wrote *Quintessence* to celebrate the orchestra's fortieth anniversary. The piece has toured thirteen cities in Europe and Australia.

Recently, there has been a marked increase in the number of commissioned works initiated by HK Phil. Through the Robert H. N. Ho Family Foundation Hong Kong Composers Scheme, workshops, mentorship and performances were organised to allow budding local composers to acquire practical knowledge and experience in music composition. On 22 and 23 November 2024, Angus Lee's . . . *aux cendres*, which came out of the scheme, was given its world premiere by the orchestra under the direction of Elim Chan.

Photo 45.3: The 'Metaverse' Symphony in 2023.

In the past, the orchestra's commissioned and premiered works were usually shorter. However, in recent years, the practice has changed. In May 2023, a whole concert was dedicated to the young composer Elliot Leung's works. There were two world premieres, including his first symphony, entitled 'Metaverse'. The programme was performed three times – an arrangement which may not have happened before (with a concert of only new works by a local composer).

From the Doming Lam concert in 1965 to Elliot Leung's concerts in 2023; from a local work being once in a blue moon during the SBO years to the HK Phil music library having hundreds of works by local composers – it has been a long journey. In different times, the orchestra has had different degrees of enthusiasm for championing works by Hong Kong composers. Opinions are divided as to how frequently HK Phil should play local works and how these works should be presented. In any case, as Hong Kong's flagship orchestra, HK Phil has taken a fair share in the promotion of our own opuses. More than that, the orchestra could be more progressive than to just play a new Hong Kong piece. What about giving it a second or third show? What can be done to package and market those new works creatively and effectively? How should the orchestra cultivate the audience's love and support of local compositions? There are questions that are worth pondering over.

46 *Half of Chan Wing Wah's Symphonic Opuses*

Very few composers since Beethoven have written a tenth symphony. One of them is from Hong Kong – Chan Wing Wah. HK Phil has played five out of the ten!

No. 1 (1979) was not a formal performance. When Ling Tung was music director, the orchestra arranged a reading session of works by Hong Kong composers. Chan Wing Wah was the only student in the group. Two movements from his first symphony were played.

No. 2 (1981) was part of his master's thesis. Doming Lam recommended the work to the orchestra, which subsequently performed it. The composer was studying in Canada and did not manage to be there at the world premiere. However, through repeatedly listening to the recording on cassette tape, he was able to learn how to achieve desirable effects.

No. 3 (1985), written for double orchestra, was part of his doctoral thesis.

No. 5 'The Three Kingdoms' (1995) was also written for double orchestra. Chan Wing Wah was HK Phil's composer-in-residence then.

No. 6 'Reunification' (1996) was written to mark Hong Kong's handover. The finale was subsequently arranged into a version with solo voice, chorus and orchestra, entitled 'Nine Regions Sing as One'.

Chan Wing Wah said, 'I had never met David Atherton, but he invited me to be composer-in-residence. At first, I thought he wanted me to write some small pieces. Later, I learned that he was thinking about pieces which last for the length of half a concert! I was also commissioned to write chamber music for a concert of entirely my works. The residency lasted for three years. The maestro encouraged me to conduct my own pieces too. All those rare opportunities afforded me enough time to understand and improve my works.'

Photo 46.1: A young Chan Wing Wah, captured during his early years as a composer.

47 *Musical Farmer*

> I like performing in school education concerts. Intrigued by music of different periods and styles, adorable kids allow seeds to be planted and germinate in the their hearts. My duty is like a farmer – to work hard in the field. Some of them may grow up to become performers like us. Even if they just learn to appreciate music, the process has allowed them to cultivate a taste for the good things in life.
>
> – Homer Lee (HK Phil's third horn)

I could not agree more with Homer's remarks. Promoting music carries much resemblance to what an industrious farmer does. One difference is that a farmer's work yields a harvest (bountiful or not), but to cultivate an interest in music is more to do with sowing the seeds and nourishing growth than witnessing a harvest. The end result may not be easily recognised. Having said that, it is vital to build a sustainable audience for classical music. Good music enhances a good quality of life. It takes unceasing efforts to introduce music to people of different ages and backgrounds. This is fundamental for the orchestra's healthy development. It is a long-range investment, and an indispensable one indeed.

In the 1950s, when SBO rehearsed at the Diocesan Boys' School, the school's students were allowed to attend the rehearsals. Sometimes the orchestra arranged promotional concerts with students as the target audience, but these were isolated cases. When professional venues opened, and when more resources were available, such educational activities were organised more systematically.

In March 1962, the LPO unveiled City Hall with a series of concerts. One month later, the pre-professional HK Phil gave their first performance at the new venue, presenting Handel's *Messiah*. The audience loved it. In years to follow, the oratorio became an annual event, taking place on Palm Sundays. The orchestra also performed a few other times a year at City Hall, with regular support from audiences.

Opportunity and Challenge

According to Darwin Chen, who was City Hall's manager then, this new cultural landmark brought both opportunities and threats. Now there was a professional venue with good sound, air-conditioning, and a perfect location. Musicians and audiences were both having a good time. That said, one big hurdle to overcome was filling the house. The concert hall alone had about 1,500 seats. Although the London Philharmonic would easily ensure a sold-out concert, it was not possible for ensembles of that calibre to come every week. At that time, classical music was very much a minority interest. There was a pressing need for audience development.

Music for All

In 1965, advocated by Darwin Chen, the Urban Council introduced a promotional concert series, and HK Phil was one of the key players among other organisations and solo performers. All tickets were sold at HK$1, making it possible for anyone to have a taste of classical music. In those years, not all of the works performed were familiar to audiences. For instance, the concert on 3 March 1968 began with Mozart's Overture to *Don Giovanni*, followed by Rachmaninov's Piano Concerto no. 2 and Beethoven's Symphony no. 3, 'Eroica'. For the concert on 19 May, there was just one long piece – Verdi's Requiem. Darwin Chen explained, 'To many, these may not be the easy-listening type of works, but the essence of these HK$1 concerts was to popularise the medium, allowing the general public to have an encounter with an orchestra.'

Photo 47.1: City Hall's manager Darwin Chen (left) and Doming Lam (right) inside City Hall Concert Hall. Courtesy of Kathy Lam.

After turning professional in 1974, the orchestra had increased resources to perform more frequently, and had more capacity (and needs!) to cultivate new listeners. In the first season, on top of concerts with full-length symphonies, the orchestra introduced a series of ten promenade concerts with shorter, more melodious works such as *Blue Danube Waltz*, *Carmen Suite*, *Jamaican Rumba*, *Pizzicato Polka*, and *Dance of the Hours*. Audiences were also treated to Chinese pieces including *Sinkiang Dance*, *White Hair Girl*, *Ka Ta Mei Ling*, and *Sum Che Tak Ma*.

More New Venues

In the early professional years, the orchestra's concerts were mostly presented by the Urban Council. With the booming of Hong Kong's economy in the 1970s, HK Phil developed at a quicker pace. More resources could be utilised for publicity, education, and public relations work. These duties slowly fell onto the hands of the orchestra.

At the same time, a new hall opened at Baptist College in Kowloon Tong. The government was also planning to build more venues such as town halls in Tsuen Wan, Sha Tin, and Tuen Mun – alongside Hong Kong Coliseum and the Cultural Centre. There was a pressing need to attract more people into concert halls. In the mid-1980s, as the Cultural Centre[1] was about to open, Assistant General Manager (Development and Marketing) Tseng Sun-man successfully advocated for the creation of a new post to coordinate audience development. Soon it became a team.

Over the years, HK Phil has committed to cultivating audience. There are at least three objectives behind these initiatives.

1. Encounter

HK Phil organises popular concerts (including popular classics and popular programmes) to let potential audiences have a taste of orchestral music. The categories include school, family, community, and inclusive concerts. Venues can be, but are not limited to, school halls, the Cultural Centre, stadiums, and the Central Waterfront. In terms of programming, a wide range of repertoire is included. Here are some examples:

- A concert of works by a single well-known composer such as Mozart, Beethoven or Tchaikovsky.
- Different types of music such as Broadway, Chinese works, folk songs (Wang Luobin's works for instance), movie music, theme songs from soap operas, overtures, ballet music, opera choruses, and music from the Romantic and Baroque periods.
- Works related to a non-musical theme such as Valentine's Day concerts, A Mid-Autumn Rendezvous in 1989 with works all related to autumn, or the moon:

[1] The capacity of its concert hall is 50% more than that of City Hall Concert Hall.

    - ⌘ Autumn: *Autumn Leaves,* Autumn from Vivaldi's *Four Seasons*, and Glazunov's *Seasons*.
    - ⌘ Moon: Debussy's *Clair de Lune*, instrumental arrangements of popular songs including *Moon River*, Teresa Tang's favourite 月亮代表我的心 ('The Moon Represents My Heart), and 月半小夜曲 ('Half Moon Serenade') by Hacken Lee (or more accurately Naoko Kawai).
- *Hooked on Classics* was a record album launched in 1981. The idea of presenting medleys of classical music melodies to disco beats had a broad appeal. HK Phil organised Get Hooked on Classics concerts in 1984. The image on the poster looked quite similar to the LP cover!
- French pianist Richard Clayderman in concert, playing his own distinctive easy-listening romantic tunes.
- Concerts with pop singers.

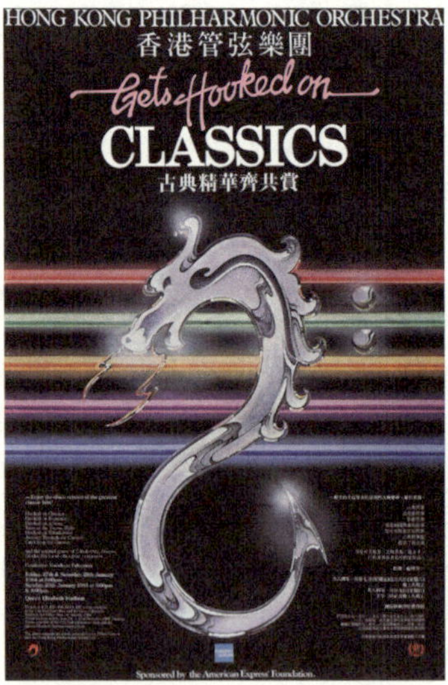

Photo 47.2 and Photo 47.3: Posters of concerts Gets Hooked on Classics and Richard Clayderman in Concert.

Open Rehearsal

Some encounters may not necessarily be showcasing popular classics. From the 2023/24 season, the orchestra has hosted the Swire Music for Everyone Series. These are the open rehearsals of regular concerts. A host offers listening tips beforehand so that audience members know what to listen out for, and what to look out for during the performance.

Close Encounters

The most direct contact audience members can have with the orchestra is if both parties share the same stage. School kids have sung and danced along to music played by the orchestra. Music students have been invited to play side-by-side with professional players in concerts. It is an eye-opener to be able to perform with HK Phil. It widens their artistic horizons and is an enriching life experience.

Adults were invited to perform with the orchestra too. On 13 January 2024, choral aficionados were invited to take part in a grand performance. This was the appeal on HK Phil's website:

> The HK Phil cordially invites all local vocal enthusiasts to join a sing-along session of Beethoven's famous finale from the Ninth Symphony! Sing the memorable lines from Schiller's *Ode to Joy* with the fellow choristers, with full support from the orchestra, soloists and chorus. The open rehearsal starts at 3 p.m., and the orchestra session begins at 5 p.m. You will be surrounded by audience members who are also choristers!

On top of being there at concerts, there are other ways to be in touch with music. HK Phil's early recordings included quite a few easy-listening works such as *Butterfly Lovers' Concerto* and *Colourful Clouds Chasing the Moon*. In the 1990s, HK Phil was involved with the productions of educational videos – 喜怒哀樂管弦樂 ('The Symphony of Emotions: Joy, Anger, Sorrow, and Happiness') and *The Carnival of the Animals*. The former linked music with emotions, and the latter was a cute music video. These video tapes were distributed freely to all primary and secondary schools via the Education Department. Recently, the orchestra has actively promoted their YouTube channel, the 'Watch & Listen' section on HK Phil's website, and simulcasts of the Swire Symphony Under the Stars, among other endeavours. As such, more people can appreciate HK Phil's music-making.

> For many years, HK Phil has provided music teachers with a wealth of teaching resources. The most practical is the introduction of instruments, especially with the video 喜怒哀樂管弦樂. In the olden days, educational software was difficult to obtain. I played that video tape to all classes. Luckily, the tape is still in good condition. During COVID, HK Phil's 'Watch & Listen' on its website made it easy for everyone to appreciate high-quality performances. No doubt, such initiatives help to reach more music lovers.
>
> – Jacqueline Liu (Former Vice-Principal and Music Panel, the Hong Kong Taoist Association Ching Chung Secondary School)

2. Discovery

Many agree that acquiring relevant knowledge about a piece makes the listening experience more meaningful. The composer's biography, information about the performers, the work's background, style of composition, and use of instruments all aid in deepening one's understanding of the piece. For this reason, at most HK Phil concerts, information about works and performers are included in a programme – something one generally will not find at a Cantopop concert.

The orchestra has done a lot to enhance audience members' musical knowledge:

- Organising pre-concert and general music appreciation talks.
- Engaging an emcee, or the conductor, to introduce the programme in family, community, festival, and educational concerts.
- Publishing music appreciation books (some series, including *Classical Period*, *Romantic Period*, *Enjoyment of Orchestral Music*, and *Russian Music*, with accompanying CDs/cassette tapes).
- Producing posters of the four families of instruments for schools to put up in music rooms.
- Presenting special music appreciation concerts hosted by the conductor or emcee.
- Organising educational projects such as Hang Seng Bank Blossom with Music, HSBC Insurance Creative Notes, and Jockey Club Keys to Music Education Programmes.
- Publishing the Music Smart series (booklets with CD, stationery and stickers) for use by students and teachers.
- Putting up online introductions of instruments by HK Phil players.

> The educational booklets were ideal companions to music lessons. After the teacher's presentation, students can read the booklet at home to enrich their understanding; this was also in line with the school's efforts to promote reading culture . . . music teachers should make use of the opportunities to take part in some high-standard educational

> initiatives. After all, individual schools may not be capable to organize such music activities singlehandedly.
>
> – Esther Chan (Former Music Panel, SKH Bishop Mok Sau Tseng Secondary School)

3. Networking

Classical music is not 'high art' and should not be perceived as such. It is a form of music that can be appreciated by everyone. Hence, it has always been in the orchestra's commitment and mandate to reach out, and make wider and deeper connections through the following means:

– Issuing of student tickets to connect with young audience members, some of whom may become HK Phil's loyal listeners. According to a veteran music teacher, it is important to let classical music be part of students' upbringing. Encouraging them to attend concerts will help make it a habit that can bring lifelong benefits.

> After finishing my Certificate of Education Examinations, I was rather free. By status, I was still a student – I took advantage of paying an affordable price to see HK Phil's concerts. To my surprise, I realised that student tickets were half-price off ALL categories! I did not have to sit at the back, or at the side. For that reason, I attended nearly all HK Phil concerts in those few months – a catalyst in helping me become a classical music maniac!
>
> – Leon Chu, choral conductor

– Setting up the Friends of the Philharmonic Society[2] and Club Bravo, to stay connected with audience members, music-lovers,

[2] Tseng Sun-man was inspired by examples set by some overseas orchestras, and recommended that the management inaugurate a similar establishment in Hong Kong.

and subscribers. On top of ticket discounts, members were also invited to meet with musicians and attend open rehearsals.

- The Tung Foundation – Young Audience Scheme provides free tickets and ticket discounts to youngsters and their families. As performers and observers, members can take part in masterclasses hosted by HK Phil musicians. Players also actively participate in educational work by providing professional coaching for school orchestras and bands.
- Fostering a good working relationship with sponsors, subtly enhancing the branding of both the sponsoring body and HK Phil.
- Performing in public and a variety of venues to engage with different communities.
- Taking part in pop concerts to connect with different audiences.
- In 1991, HK Phil co-organised a music critic programme with the department of Extramural Studies at The Chinese University of Hong Kong. Veteran music critics including Lai Kin, Chow Fan-fu, and Ip Shun-chi were instructors. That reflected the orchestra's efforts to connect with those interested in music criticism and aesthetics.

Photo 47.4: Young Audience Scheme.

Photo 47.5: Jockey Club Keys to Music Education Programme Activity Book.

I could go on forever about the orchestra's networking efforts! Feel free to go back to the previous chapters 'Made for Each Other' and 'How "Hong Kong" is the Phil?' for reference.

I mention in the beginning of this chapter that with audience development, it is not easy to witness a harvest. However, if we compare HK Phil's audiences today to those of the early professional years, it is not difficult to spot some marked differences: the audience size has grown tremendously, while the average age of concert attendants has dropped significantly. There are quite a lot of veteran listeners now, and audiences in general are more open to music of different styles. These are encouraging phenomena. Special thanks should be given to all who have played a part in sowing the seeds for the development of classical music in Hong Kong. Among them are the two music teachers mentioned earlier, as well as the following subscriber . . .

Photo 47.6: Jockey Club TUTTI Programme: Share the Stage with Maestro Christoph Eschenbach – Conducting Masterclass in 2024. HK Phil players were joined by local young instrumentalists and conductors while being coached by one of the world's most distinguished maestros.

48 *The School Supervisor Who Oversubscribes*

Mr Tin Wing-sin started subscribing to HK Phil's concerts at the beginning of the 1990s. He buys tickets to every concert. On top of that, he picks six programmes of easier-listening works every year and books two more tickets each. As school supervisor of Tin Ka Ping Secondary School, he would then ask the school's music teacher to nominate two students each time to join him in attending a HK Phil concert. On the day, the two lucky ones will have a dinner with the school supervisor. Over the meal, Mr Tin will brief them on concert etiquette and listen to the students talking about school life. No concert reports are required. The two students just sit back and enjoy the music to its fullest. After the show, Mr Tin becomes their chauffeur and drives them home.

As always, Supervisor Tin treasures spending time with students, and feels grateful to be able to bring the classical concert experience, a pleasurable thing in life, to youngsters. Mr Tin recalls bumping into those students again. They may already be working, married, or have children, but many still recall the time when they attended a concert with Mr Tin. There have been hundreds of them, and quite often the supervisor may not be able to recognise them. Yet it is always heartwarming to know that they still remember that special musical moment.

Mr Tin is a dedicated music-lover. Probably, he is also one of very few school supervisors interested in audience development.

Photo 48.1: The oversubscribing supervisor, along with students Huang Yuyuan Claire (middle) and Zhan Kai Ying Kelly (right) from Tin Ka Ping Secondary School, attended a HK Phil concert in September 2024. It was Kelly's first classical concert experience and the programme included Stravinsky's *The Rite of Spring*. She liked it! Courtesy of Tin Wing-sin.

49 *Guinness World Record*

One way to be in touch with the orchestra is to perform with it! The more performers the better! How about creating a world record together? 13 November 2009 was the big day for another Swire Symphony Under the Stars, which took place at the Happy Valley Sports Ground. HK Phil, Tom Lee Music, and the Hong Kong Harmonica Association (HKHA) came together in an attempt to break a world record. At twilight, HKHA's Vice-Chairman Rocky Lok first taught everyone how to play the harmonica! There was no shortage of absolute beginners in the crowd. Luckily, most players on site used special harmonicas provided by Tom Lee Music. There were only four big holes on the instrument. In fact, it was not easy to play a wrong note. At the real show, a total of 6,131 people took part in the performance. The piece was very accessible – everyone became a performer! The total playing time was seven minutes and twenty-five seconds. Everything went smoothly, and everyone had a great time. That may also have been the biggest crowd of instrumentalists which HK Phil has accompanied. As of the printing deadline of this book, the Guinness World Record for the Largest Harmonica Ensemble set that evening remains unbroken!

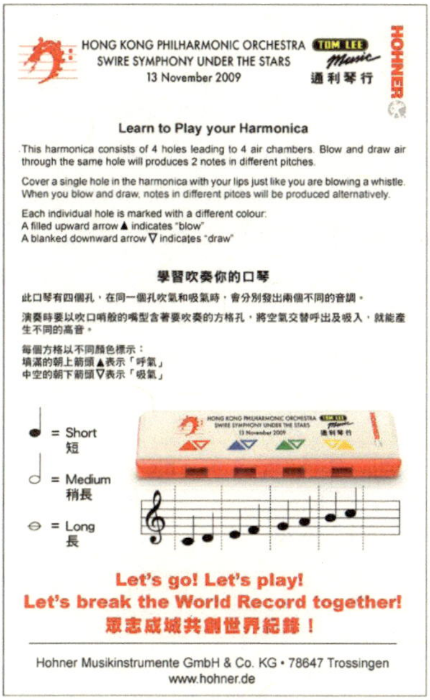

Photo 49.1 and Photo 49.2: Most audience members used this music score and the cute little harmonica at the record-breaking performance.

50 *Words from the Aficionados*

While writing this book, I had the honour of chatting with some seventy people. Among them were HK Phil players, conductors, soloists, arts administrators, music critics, academics, and audience members. Their backgrounds vary, but they share something in common – a passion for music. I was greatly impressed by their sincerity and excitement while they shared their intriguing stories, insights on music, and quotable quotes. With limited space, I can only excerpt a small part of it.

The Heart of the Conductor

Jaap van Zweden told Fan Ting, 'If you want to be a conductor, you have to be like me – shelve your violin!'

Pavarotti Sang Especially for Me

In 2005, Luciano Pavarotti shared the stage with the Phil. During rehearsal, the tenor felt that something was not right with the clarinet solo in the aria *E lucevan le stelle*. Andrew Simon said, 'In front of the conductor, all other players and colleagues, he sang the melody once to ME; and made a remark which I find useful to this day, "more distance, less square!"'

The Concertmaster's Showtime

One major duty of the concertmaster is to play solo passages. Jing Wang has this to say, 'There are some big solo cadenzas in *Scheherazade*, where I am basically on my own, and I just have to play well. With *Ein Heldenleben*, however, it is a different story. Often, I have to work closely with the horn solo, although we are wide apart on stage. This is also the case with the ending of the second movement in Brahms's Symphony no. 1.'

Jaap and Tarmo

Jonathan Van Dyke: 'As conductors, Jaap and Tarmo are of two contrasting styles. Tarmo allows different tempos, phrasings, and colours on different nights. He gives the players much more freedom. Whereas Jaap likes to dictate, for example, how each note of the oboe cadenza in the first movement of Beethoven Fifth is to be executed.'

Rachel and Rubinstein

Edo de Waart once told Rachel Cheung, 'Among the soloists I have worked with, you are the youngest . . . the eldest's name was Arthur Rubinstein!'

Let Go

David Atherton shared a word about conducting with Yip Wing-sie, 'There is no need to drill unceasingly on a certain spot. Players need some time to internalise and respond to what the conductor wants. You have to know when to let go.'

Auditioning Lim Kek-tjiang

One afternoon in 1968, Lim Kek-tjiang brought along his violin to Darwin Chen's office at City Hall. He had moved to Hong Kong not long ago and was hoping to find his fortune.

Darwin recalls, 'I asked Lim, would you like to play something for me? Lim then played some Bach. It was good! Then I asked if he had played concertos? He answered with a question, "Which one do you want to hear?" I like the Beethoven concerto, and since there was no accompanist, I requested the first movement's cadenza . . . it was played so well. Like that, I told him to consider working with the Hong Kong Philharmonic Orchestra.'

When HK Phil turned professional, Darwin Chen was the first chairman of the Management Sub-committee, and Lim Kek-tjiang was the first music director.

Big Works and New Works

Former violinist Lee Wai-fook: 'We seldom played works by Bruckner, Mahler or Richard Strauss. Each performance of their works represented a learning opportunity . . . while Ling Tung was a champion of the French repertoire, he also introduced quite a few works by contemporary composers, for example Copland.'

Hisaishi +

Long-time audience member Eric Li: 'I hope when Joe Hisaishi comes next time, on top of his own works, he can conduct other classical works. He brought Shostakovich Fifth to Taiwan, Ravel to Singapore, and Schumann to Macau.'

The Most Unprofessional Player

The workforce was small when HK Phil first turned professional. Office Assistant Ambrose Law had to look after rehearsals too. His wide range of duties included setting up chairs, taking attendance, and unfolding and folding dozens of music stands. One extra assignment twisted his fate.

Ambrose casts his mind back to that particular rehearsal:

> We were always short of percussionists. One quick solution was to ask someone to cover the part. After a few string players had tried hitting the bass drum in the Shostakovich 5, the effect was still unsatisfactory. Seeing that I was sitting around doing nothing, the conductor Lim Kek-tjiang asked me to give it a go. He knew I used to play the flute at school band and could read music. With absolutely no knowledge of the percussion, I bit the bullet and went over to ask Ra Ki-bok, the timpani player, which part of the drum was I supposed to hit. In effect, I did not even know how to hold the mallet. Unexpectedly, that 'open audition' went quite well. The whole orchestra applauded and stomped their feet to express their approval. As simple as that, I took part in the real performances and became the most unprofessional player on stage.

The story continued like a Korean drama. That adventure was an eye-opener to Ambrose. In no time, he quickly made Ra Ki-bok his teacher and started learning from scratch how to play different percussion instruments. He worked really hard while continuing to take part in the orchestra's performances. Until the early 1980s, he was a regular freelance percussionist, absolutely professional!

During his performance career, one particular piece has brought him an everlasting memory: 'In those days, resources were scarce. We played Britten's *The Young Person's Guide to the Orchestra* with only two percussionists and the timpanist. One instrument here, one instrument there, one hanging on the music stand, and one at the back of my hand. Despite the mess and stress, all went well in the end.'

Vibrato

Jing Wang: 'Fifty percent of the time Jaap spent on string players was on vibrato . . . we all know there are different types of vibratos, but a string player really needs to know which muscles are to be used to master those vibratos . . . some players overlook the importance of vibrating the note "before" shifting positions. This would affect the phrasing.'

Edo's Repertoire

Co-Principal Trumpet Christopher Moyse: 'With a long career, Edo has built a huge repertoire. He brought some less frequently heard works to Hong Kong like Elgar's Symphony no. 2, quite a few John Adams works, and Walton's *Henry V*, with choir and narration.'

Grit

Fan Ting: 'If a tutti player does not play with drive, his or her technique will deteriorate. So, always give your best!'

Board Chairman = Die-Hard Fan

Y. S. Liu was a dedicated HK Phil Board chairman who always strived to solve players' problems. He says, 'I saw myself as a father figure. Once I spoke to a player who walked out of a rehearsal in disagreement with a guest conductor!' He was a super-loyal HK Phil listener too. When he was chairman, he attended all HK Phil concerts – often both nights of the same programme, except when he was not in Hong Kong, or sick. He recalls, 'Whenever I did not show up at a concert, the day after, some players would ask me why!'

Record Holder

Andrew Simon is not the longest-serving player in the orchestra. However, he may have played the most number of works (and performances) that feature the clarinet and orchestra.

Andrew Simon: 'Let me count . . . Richard Tsang, Artie Shaw, Mendelssohn, Mozart, Weber 1 and 2, Rossini, Debussy, Finzi, Bernstein, Stamitz, Martin, Copland, Corigliano, Mozart's Sinfonia Concertante, Brossé (with the composer conducting), Baermann, Stravinsky, Lutosławski . . . Oh, and Ponchielli, too!'

The Applause Was More Thrilling

Words by HK Phil's longest-serving musician Homer Lee: 'In the past thirty-seven years, I have taken part in countless truly remarkable performances playing orchestral works, operas, ballets, movie music, and pop music. We touch the audience's hearts, and they touch ours! Their applause, which fills the concert hall, is more thrilling to us than the music.'

Same School

Jing Wang: 'Jaap and I both studied at Juilliard. We went through the same Juilliard system of teaching. I know exactly what he wants, and I can effectively communicate with fellow players on how Jaap's desirable sound can be produced.'

Between Business and Music

David Gwilt, member of the General Committee: 'The General Committee at the time was made up of largely successful businessmen of various kinds, with strong ideas on how to run businesses but with no experience in dealing with musicians, so when personnel problems arose, their response tended to be "if you don't like it, leave!" I was a moderating influence between the Committee and the players on such occasions.'

Why HK Phil?

Opera producer Lo King-man: 'Between 1968 and 2004, when I produced large-scale operas annually, HK Phil was my regular partner. The orchestra already had a long history and a professional level of playing then. They were capable of sustaining a high and consistent performance standard, which was in line with my plan to involve professional singers from the international scene. In those days, the Urban Council supported my productions. They also supported HK Phil. Working with HK Phil was a reasonable arrangement.'

The Ring in Progression

Jing Wang: 'For the *Ring*, the learning process has to be spread out. You can't just swallow everything in one go.'

HK Phil presented the four parts of Wagner's *Ring* cycle in four years. Jonathan Van Dyke reflects, 'Listening back to the four parts of the *Ring* cycle, one can easily feel that the sound has developed progressively. For *Das Rheingold*, the learning curve was steep. However, once we have gotten used to the leitmotifs, pacing, and the Wagner crescendo (which can last for five minutes), we sounded better and better.'

Play from Memory

Tchaikovsky's Symphony no. 5 was in the programme of the first professional concert in 1974. How intense was the rehearsal?

Fan Ting: 'Lim Kek-tjiang made all string players memorise the coda. At first, everyone was immensely stressed. During the real show, however, we played perfectly.'

Comrades

Andrew Simon: 'Colleagues are like partners in trenches.'

Each Second Counts

Kenneth Jean shared a little tip with Yip Wing-sie on directing a student concert: 'There are usually many short excerpts. You have to flip to the right pages and stack up the pile of scores. For a student concert, a few seconds to turn pages and replace scores is too long!'

One Hall Two Impressions

Jonathan Van Dyke: 'The sound of the Cultural Centre Concert Hall does not favour the double-bass section. In order to create clean articulation despite the muddy acoustics, we have to prioritise playing with a powerful projecting tone. When we performed at Musikverein and Tonhalle Zürich, we were able to create the same amount of sound with much less effort so we could concentrate on making a more beautiful tone.'

Jing Wang also likes the sound of those two halls. About Cultural Centre, he said: 'Its acoustics are great for the upper strings. I do not have to try too hard to project my solo lines.'

A Highly Mouldable Ensemble

Leung Kin-fung: 'HK Phil is especially mouldable – we respond very quickly to conductors. In other words, under a different conductor, we become a different ensemble. This is not the case with some Japanese and German orchestras. However, it may not be a good thing – when we work with a mediocre conductor, our performance becomes mediocre.'

Clever Programming

Eric Li: 'David Atherton planned his programmes strategically. He paired Mozart with Stravinsky. Distinguished musicians like violinist William Preucil and cellist Lynn Harrell were invited to play concertos and chamber music in the same concert. Pianists Peter Donohoe's complete Rachmaninov concertos and John Lill's complete Beethoven concertos were eye-openers! Audience found favour with these clever programmes and expanded their listening horizons.'

An Exceptional Brain

Leung Kin-fung: 'Lorin Maazel was awesome. He could give totally different instructions with his left and right hands at the same time!'

Learning to Say No

Yip Wing-sie was once considering accepting an outside engagement. David Atherton told her to ask herself three questions, 'Do you really want to accept the invitation? Will it bring you artistic benefits? Do you need the money?' This process of reflection helped her make further artistic decisions in her career.

Sweat of Professionalism

Fan Ting: 'Joshua Bell has played the Tchaikovsky Concerto innumerable times. A few days before coming to Hong Kong, he just did it again in Israel. I sat behind him and saw that he played with all his might, although it was just a rehearsal. The air-conditioning was in full power, yet sweat came rolling down his arm. That's professionalism!'

Sound from the Back

Leung Kin-fung: 'Jaap changed our concept of sound. One way to achieve that new sound was to ask the players at the back desks to play louder and to take more initiative. He likes the sound to envelop from the back.'

Jing Wang feels it: 'He always asks Andrew Ling [principal viola] and Richard Bamping [principal cello] to play less and demands that the back desks play more. To front desk players, this helped them feel the support from the back.'

Jonathan Van Dyke remembers Jaap asking, 'Do you know why Porsche makes the best cars? That's because they put the engine at the back.'

Underaged Player

Lo King-man:

> In 1953, I was a 15-year-old student at Diocesan Boys' School. The school has a rich music culture which inspired me to learn an instrument. Father's friend Dr C. K. Wong was a member of SBO. People addressed him as 'King of Dongxiao'. He excelled in Western and Chinese music, playing both the flute and *dongxiao* brilliantly. He recommended that I take up the French horn. When members of the amateur SBO knew I was interested in learning to play the 'uncommon' instrument, they bought me one. They also found me a teacher who was a military officer based in Shek Kong. The condition was that I should join SBO when I had mastered the skills. I kept my promise and joined the orchestra about six weeks after my first lesson. I remained a horn player in SBO, and later HK Phil. I left in 1969 to focus on my full-time work at HKU and commitment to the development of opera. During my days at the orchestras, rehearsals were held on Wednesdays. There was no fee. Each player got a cup of tea and a piece of cake, though.

Jaap's Favourite

Fan Ting: 'Jaap really loves Beethoven's Fifth. In Shanghai, we played the first movement as an encore! . . . and before the finale, he instructed us to play a quick down-bow, and a slow up-bow with no vibrato. We sounded like one voice. It was powerful!'

The Conductor Least Interested in Details

David Gwilt: 'Schermerhorn knew how to build climax. The orchestra was not technically accomplished, but he had vast experience with dance and hence was capable of creating rhythmic excitement. He was least interested in detail, but his music was full of drive.'

HK Phil in the Eyes of the Concertmaster

Jing Wang has been HK Phil's concertmaster for twelve years, making him the longest serving concertmaster in the orchestra's history. He previously led the Dallas Opera Orchestra in the same position for three years. Jing has also been guest concertmaster for quite a few orchestras. In his opinion, HK Phil is definitely of the best international standard, 'The management is good, the committee is dedicated, and HK Phil excels artistically. Players are well prepared every week for both shows on Fridays and Saturdays, ready to give their 200% . . . Actions speak louder than words!'

Heart of the Trumpeter

Christopher Moyse: 'I appreciate colleagues' "childish enthusiasm" with music. Take Andrew Simon and Jarod Vermette for instance. You feel that freshness when they open up their cases, that steadfast mindset of "the show must go on", and the level of freedom . . . They play without inhibition. I hope I can have that level of enthusiasm when I've been doing it as long as they have. I will try to keep enjoying it, counting my blessings that I'll be able to do it!'

– The End –

Epilogue: Back Where We Began

Photo 51.1: SBO in 1948.

This postlude reminds me of our first chord!

Take another look at this photo, which was taken at the SBO's first concert at St. Stephen's Girls' School. The date was 30 April 1948. It was more than an orchestral concert, with piano solo (Beethoven's 'Appassionata' Sonata), some solo singing (with piano accompaniment), Mozart's *Marriage of Figaro* Overture, and Haydn's Symphony no. 4 in D major, 'The Clock'.

SINO-BRITISH CLUB—MUSIC GROUP

中英學會—音樂組

FIFTH CONCERT

at

St. Stephen's Girls' College
Hong Kong

on

Friday, 30th April, 1948
at 8.30 p.m.

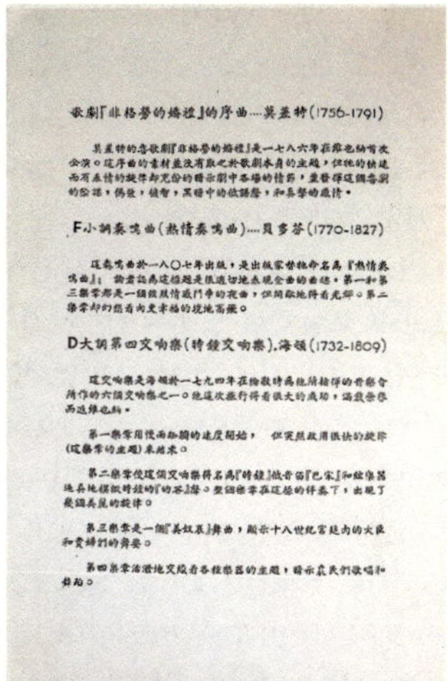

歌劇『非格勞的婚禮』的序曲....莫差特(1756-1791)

莫差特的喜歌劇『非格勞的婚禮』是一七八六年在維也納首次公演。這序曲的素材並沒有取之於歌劇本身的主題，但牠的快捷而有熱情的旋律卻充份的暗示劇中各場的情節，並替得這個喜劇的紛擾，偽裝，詭智，黑暗中的低語聲，和真摯的感情。

F小調奏鳴曲(熱情奏鳴曲)....貝多芬(1770-1827)

這奏鳴曲於一八〇七年出版，是出版家替牠命名為『熱情奏鳴曲』；論者認為這標題是很適切地表現全曲的曲趣。第一和第三樂章都是一個銳烈情感鬥爭的夜曲，但間歇地得看光輝。第二樂章卻約略看向更幸福的境地高飛。

D大調第四交响樂(時鐘交响樂).海頓(1732-1809)

這交響樂是海頓於一七九四年在倫敦時為他所指揮的音樂會所作的六個交響樂之一。他這次旅行得着很大的成功，滿載榮譽而返維也納。

第一樂章用慢而和諧的速度開始，但突然改用很快的旋律(這樂章的主題)來結束。

第二樂章使這個交響樂得名為『時鐘』低音的『巴宋』和絃樂器連長地模倣時鐘的『的答』聲。整個樂章在這樣的伴奏下，出現了優雅美麗的旋律。

第三樂章是一個『美奴愛』舞曲，顯示十八世紀宮廷內的大使和貴婦們的舞姿。

第四樂章活潑地交織着各種樂器的主題，暗示農民們歌唱和舞蹈。

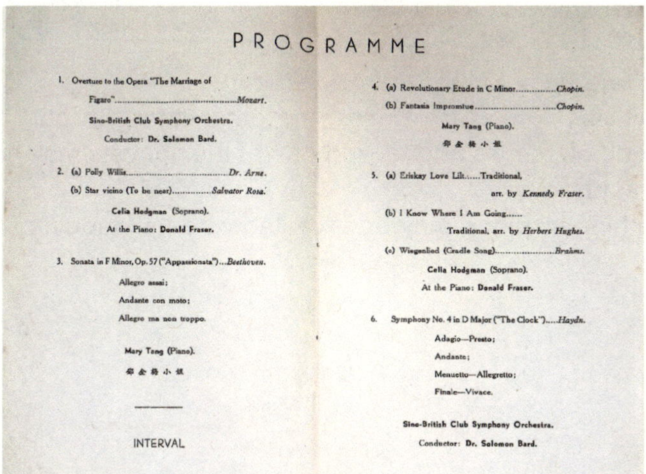

PROGRAMME

1. Overture to the Opera "The Marriage of Figaro"..........*Mozart.*
   Sino-British Club Symphony Orchestra.
   Conductor: **Dr. Solomon Bard.**

2. (a) Polly Willis..........*Dr. Arne.*
   (b) Star vicino (To be near)..........*Salvator Rosa.*
   Celia Hodgman (Soprano).
   At the Piano: **Donald Fraser.**

3. Sonata in F Minor, Op. 57 ("Appassionata")...*Beethoven.*
   Allegro assai;
   Andante con moto;
   Allegro ma non troppo.
   Mary Tang (Piano).
   鄧金娣小姐

INTERVAL

4. (a) Revolutionary Etude in C Minor..........*Chopin.*
   (b) Fantasia Impromtue..........*Chopin.*
   Mary Tang (Piano).
   鄧金娣小姐

5. (a) Eriskay Love Lilt.....Traditional, arr. by *Kennedy Fraser.*
   (b) I Know Where I Am Going...... Traditional, arr. by *Herbert Hughes.*
   (c) Wiegenlied (Cradle Song)..........*Brahms.*
   Celia Hodgman (Soprano).
   At the Piano: **Donald Fraser.**

6. Symphony No. 4 in D Major ("The Clock")....*Haydn.*
   Adagio—Presto;
   Andante;
   Menuetto—Allegretto;
   Finale—Vivace.
   Sino-British Club Symphony Orchestra.
   Conductor: **Dr. Solomon Bard.**

Photo 51.2, Photo 51.3, and Photo 51.4: House programme for SBO's first concert.

If the same programme were presented today, the 'Clock' Symphony would have been no. 101. This was merely a matter of editions. An observant music-lover may discover something else more peculiar.

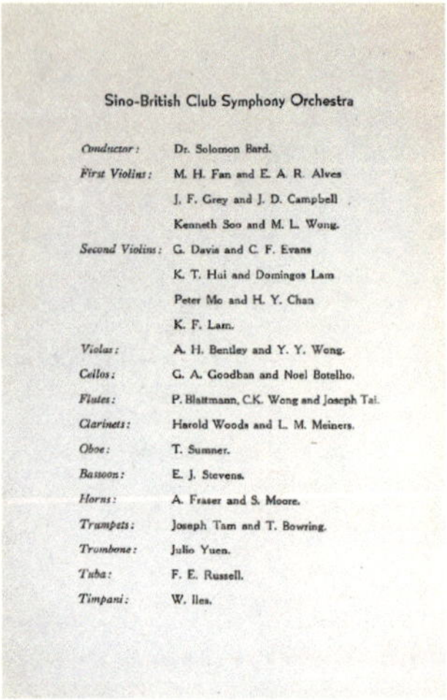

Sino-British Club Symphony Orchestra

Conductor:	Dr. Solomon Bard.
First Violins:	M. H. Fan and E. A. R. Alves
	J. F. Grey and J. D. Campbell
	Kenneth Soo and M. L. Wong.
Second Violins:	G. Davis and C. F. Evans
	K. T. Hui and Domingos Lam
	Peter Mo and H. Y. Chan
	K. F. Lam.
Violas:	A. H. Bentley and Y. Y. Wong.
Cellos:	G. A. Goodban and Noel Botelho.
Flutes:	P. Blattmann, C.K. Wong and Joseph Tai.
Clarinets:	Harold Woods and L. M. Meiners.
Oboe:	T. Sumner.
Bassoon:	E. J. Stevens.
Horns:	A. Fraser and S. Moore.
Trumpets:	Joseph Tam and T. Bowring.
Trombone:	Julio Yuen.
Tuba:	F. E. Russell.
Timpani:	W. Iles.

Photo 51.5: The orchestra member list for SBO's first concert.

First, the orchestra was missing an essential instrument, the double bass. Second, why was a tuba called for? The two orchestral works belong to the classical period of the eighteenth century. The instrument was not even invented then.

Now, look closely at the players' list. (Does the name of a second violinist – Domingos Lam – look familiar? Yes, Maestro Doming Lam, the iconic Hong Kong composer, was a founding member of the orchestra.) You may realise there was only one bassoonist, one oboist, but three flautists. Here is my guess: the other bassoon part may have been played on the trombone, and one of the flautists may have taken the second oboe part.

Something inspiring may be revealed when juxtaposing the 'then' and 'now'.

Table 51.1: A comparison of the SBO and HK Phil today

Then	Now
In a newspaper advertisement posted in October 1947, the amateur SBO appealed to musicians who knew how to play an orchestral instrument to attend their rehearsal on the 22nd at St. Joseph's College. Those interested were reminded to bring along their own music stands as the orchestra did not have such provision.	Since becoming professional in 1974, HK Phil has required players to go through competitive auditions. Today, rehearsals take place at the Cultural Centre Concert Hall, where there are plenty of music stands. More than that, one can just push it down, or pull it up to adjust the height. A light and a rack (for placing a bow or pen) can easily be attached onto the stand; and conductor stands are also provided.
Before the first concert, SBO spent 'a few' months to prepare for 'half' of a programme.	Today, HK Phil may present 'a few' programmes within 'half' a month.
For a year from April 1948, SBO gave about four concerts.	HK Phil usually has a forty-four-week season, giving more than 150 concerts.
There are thirty-one names on the players' list. However, about thirty-five musicians appeared on stage. Four may have joined the band at short notice.	HK Phil currently has ninety-six full-time players. Freelance players are sometimes called in. In the case of Richard Strauss's *An Alpine Symphony*, there were 110 players on stage, and another eight musicians who played the horn from backstage.

Source: Author.

Before World War II, Hong Kong saw scattered instances of orchestral playing (find out more in 香港音樂的前世今生 ['Music in a Bygone Era: Music Development in Hong Kong 1930s–1950s'] – a book in Chinese written by Dr Oliver Chou), but the post-war development of orchestral music pioneered by SBO and succeeded by the HK Phil was phenomenal. That premiere performance in 1948 very much started from scratch. The orchestra's 'founding fathers' truly had great vision, intelligence and perseverance.

Looking at what we have today, I am reminded of an old Chinese saying, 'One generation plants the tree, another gets the shade.' Behind this seventy-eight-year philharmonic (which, loosely, means 'the love of music') history, there is a multitude of music-loving contributors through the ages: composers, lyricists and arrangers who have left us a rich repertoire; players, soloists and conductors who transform written notes into beautiful music for listeners' pleasure; and people such as music critics, media works, arts administrators, stage professionals, donors and teachers who foster a favourable environment for orchestral music to blossom.

Some of these seasoned music-lovers became my interviewees. More than that, I continued to trouble them for fact-checking, verification, and supplementary information. They have all been generous and helpful to this tiresome writer. I found one thing in common among them: their passion for music. All my interview requests got a green light. While talking about music and the orchestra, all interviewees were enthusiastic. Even with time flying by, there were always more captivating stories to tell. I am deeply touched by their trust in me, their friendship, and their everlasting love of music.

I am also grateful to those who have left us a wealth of written words, pictures, and audio-visual records. Going through such materials was a mesmerising experience. Special credit must be given to one of my main sources of reference: 愛與音樂同行——香港管弦樂團30年 ('Music with Love – 30th Anniversary of Hong Kong Philharmonic

Orchestra'), a book in Chinese written by the late Mr Chow Fan-fu. Although he has passed away in 2021, this anthology of his continues to live on.

At this point, let me pay tribute to the late Mrs Regina Simon, who inspired her son Andrew to sponsor this publication. As I have mentioned in the chapter 'Moments of Sentiment', this book would not have come to fruition without the bond between them. I am indebted to her and Andy for demonstrating to me that love never dies.

My thanks also go especially to two veteran runners of the orchestra for taking their time to grace this publication with two high-powered messages. I vividly felt their commitment to the orchestra during our meetings. When such commitment is translated into text, it makes for a fulfilling read.

Please bear with me if I am not able to name each colleague of mine who has given me valuable advice on the presentation of my research materials. I am thankful to staff members at the orchestra's office, editors, editorial assistants, and the dedicated team at Hong Kong University Press. The book would not have come to life without their fruitful contributions.

Finally, let me quote that old Chinese saying again – 'One generation plants the tree, another gets the shade'. We count our blessings to be in the shade. As audience members, we are planters too. Our applause and appreciation are essential nutrients for the orchestra to further develop. May Hong Kong Philharmonic Orchestra continue to shine in years to come, as we continue on this magical philharmonic journey.

Jimmy Shiu
1 March 2025

Appendix

A Look Back at the HK Phil

In January 1979 I knew nothing about a professional symphony orchestra in Hong Kong. I had just completed eight happy years with the excellent Scottish Opera following a short period with the BBC in London and a First-Class Honours degree in Music. I was beginning to think I ought to consider working overseas when I learned the Hong Kong Philharmonic was about to hold interviews for the post of general manager. Making a few phone calls to friends who knew Hong Kong, I was informed I would love working there but that the orchestra might be a 'challenge' – the implication being it was an orchestra with problems and that managing it might not be plain sailing. Nevertheless, I applied.

Five weeks later on 3 March I was landing at Kai Tak airport ready to face that challenge.

For my first month, I was put up in the old Lee Gardens Hotel in Causeway Bay, long since demolished. But its location was perfect since it was only a five-minute walk down Percival Street to Harbour View Commercial Building (now also demolished) where the Philharmonic had its offices on the twentieth floor. Instantly I fell in love with my own office. From my desk, I had a view of The Peak round through Central and the soon-to-be skyscraper-dotted Admiralty and Wan Chai, across to Kowloon and, if I stretched a little, to the airport. Down in front of me across Gloucester Road was the Yacht Club and the harbour. I could not have been more happy.

Once I had heard the orchestra and attended a few concerts, I was aware there were more than a few problems to solve. Not that anyone could really be blamed for these. Starting up any professional ensemble, especially an orchestra – and even more so one with musicians not only from Hong Kong but also a large contingent making up most of the wind and brass sections from the United States – would never be easy anywhere in the world. This is particularly true when, as with the Philharmonic, many of the musicians were almost instantly changing status from amateur to professional.

One problem I found was that advance planning had ground almost to a halt. Few conductors and guest soloists had been booked for the 1979/80 season due to start in September. With most orchestras planning at least two years in advance, this made it vital that I contact the major artists' management companies in London and New York urgently. With the exception of the first professional season when an attempt had been made to sell concerts on a subscription basis, all concerts were individually marketed. This is hugely time-consuming and expensive. I was therefore determined that a new subscription scheme had to be launched. This necessitated getting artists and programmes finalised in just a matter of weeks.

My second motive for starting a subscription was a burning desire to change the balance of the audience. Most of the regular audience seemed to be expatriates. This was perhaps understandable, given that most Hong Kong residents were immigrants from China with little time for entertainment other than television and movies. But Hong Kong was quickly transforming to a global financial and trade centre. Hong Kong Chinese had already started taking over some of the old traditional Hong Kong businesses in addition to starting their own. Wealth was trickling down. I was certain many families would want to emulate others worldwide by finding out more about music and being encouraged to attend concerts.

Initially the Philharmonic's General Committee had reservations about subscription. It became clear that some members were concerned we might be creating an expat club. But my argument won the day when I agreed we would cap the number of subscriptions at just over 50% of available seats. When we achieved more than 30% subscribers, we were all elated.

Total attendees per concert, though, were always limited by the 1,450-seat capacity of the City Hall Concert Hall. That changed in December when we were invited by the Hong Kong Jockey Club to give an afternoon concert to inaugurate the infield park at the new Shatin racetrack. Here was an opportunity I craved: the chance to perform to a much larger audience. In addition to short classical works, we invited the popular Hong Kong Canto-pop singer Roman Tam to sing with us. On a beautiful December afternoon, we presented the concert to 10,000 listeners, most of whom would never have heard a symphony orchestra before.

The second half of that subscription season taking us to July 1980 was even more successful than the first. The musicians were also enjoying playing under some more experienced conductors, especially in the final three weeks of the season with the American Kenneth Schermerhorn. Ken had just resigned after a long tenure as Music Director of the Milwaukee Symphony. After one concert that orchestra had presented in New York's finest concert hall, Carnegie Hall, the influential critic of *The New Yorker* magazine, Andrew Porter, wrote, 'A superb conductor. I should place him, without further thought or qualification, among the finest conductors of any nationality now before the American public.' Little surprise, perhaps, that Ken would return to Hong Kong on a regular basis, by 1984 as music director.

The Philharmonic by 1980 was still relatively small for a symphony orchestra, having only around sixty-five musicians. I had informed the General Committee that somehow we had to find the funds to increase the size to nearer eighty-four so that the larger symphonic works could be more regularly performed. I was therefore asked to prepare a five-year plan to outline how I saw the orchestra being developed. Apart from numbers, I stressed the need for formal auditions leading to tenure, better-quality conductors and soloists engaged more regularly, the development of a more comprehensive educational programme that children attending would actually enjoy rather than merely endure, and – again – doing everything possible to change the balance of the audience.

There were several other key parts to my plan. One was the need to make the Hong Kong Philharmonic much better known outside Hong Kong. Only by doing so could we attract even better musicians and the most international of soloists. This was doubly important because the Hong Kong government had decided to spend a very large sum on building an academy for performing arts in Wan Chai, a gift from the Hong Kong Jockey Club to celebrate its hundredth anniversary. As with major orchestras everywhere, the Philharmonic's best musicians would be needed to help train the next generation of Hong Kong instrumentalists.

Very quickly fate played into my hands. Having lunch with some of London's finest orchestral musicians in the summer of 1980, Carl Pini the hugely experienced and much-admired concertmaster of London's Philharmonia Orchestra said he had heard about Hong Kong and might be interested in coming to spend a few years. Another of his colleagues from that orchestra's string section, Ben(edict) Cruft, expressed a similar view. To cut a long story short, funds were quickly found in Hong Kong to engage both musicians. It was an enormous coup that made headlines in musical journals around the world.

Carl (known to all as Tony) made an immediate impact at his first pair of concerts. The piano soloist Ilana Vered was playing the Mozart C major concerto K. 467. All had gone well at the Friday evening concert. By the Saturday afternoon Ms Vered was unwell and unable to perform. How to salvage the concert? It was much too late to fly anyone in. But Tony said he had just performed one of the Mozart violin concertos in London. If the library had the parts and the conductor felt he could lead the orchestra without rehearsal, he would be happy to perform it.

We changed the order of the concert to put the symphony in the first half. This gave the conductor, Tony, and the principals time during the intermission to quickly discuss issues like tempi and phrasing. For an orchestra which had played very little Mozart and a soloist who did not know the orchestra it was a complete triumph. The audience gave everyone a standing ovation at the end.

The following summer I was in London finding conductors and soloists for the 1982/83 and 1983/84 seasons when fate again played into our hands. We still had to find a soloist and conductor for an important Arts Festival concert in February – only eight months away. At my first meeting I was discussing this with the impresario Lilian Hochhauser when a glint appeared in her eye.

'I know exactly what you want.'

I was not aware till then that she was helping Maxim Shostakovich and his pianist son Dmitri become established in the West. The son and grandson of the great Soviet composer, they had defected only eight weeks earlier.

'Why don't you engage Maxim to conduct, Dmitri to play the Second Piano Concerto and have a Shostakovich Symphony in the second half? You will then be the only orchestra outside the Soviet Union to have three Shostakovichs on the same stage at the same time.' She laughed! I looked to the heavens with thanks! The concert was a very big success. As a result, Maxim accepted our invitation to become principal guest conductor for three seasons. Our international profile was growing steadily.

Within Asia, I had already been making regular trips to meet agents and promoters in Japan. Soon after our Shostakovich concert, I received an invitation for the Philharmonic to take part in the 1983 Osaka International Festival, then the most important music festival in Asia. Given that we would be performing in the same festival as the Washington National Symphony Orchestra under Rostropovich and the Vienna Philharmonic under Maazel, it was vitally important that the orchestra perform well. I soon added a pair of concerts in Singapore and Bangkok before Osaka, and as soloist engaged the great Polish violinist Ida Haendel, who performed a glorious Brahms Violin Concerto. I invited Ken Schermerhorn to return to conduct what was a very happy tour. Having taken some Hong Kong journalists with us, the orchestra's triumph in Osaka was made known to the Hong Kong public.

Back in our home base in the City Hall Concert Hall, we had devoted one half season subscription to much more twentieth century music by composers like Berio, Penderecki, and Lutosławski. I brought the Scottish composer Thea Musgrave to conduct her horn concerto with Barry Tuckwell as soloist, the player for whom the work had been written. I was quite surprised to find that audience numbers did not fall off. Still our roster of conductors and soloists showed how international the orchestra was becoming. Sir Alexander Gibson, Sir Charles Groves, Sir Edward Downes, Myung-whun Chung, Gerard Schwarz, Gidon Kremer, Earl Wild, Rudolf Firkušný, Stephen Hough and others graced the stage with us.

While classical concerts were always our staple 'bread and butter', I owe a major debt of gratitude to the former Legislative Councillor Selina Chow. In 1982 she was running her own entertainment company and planning a series of concerts in the Queen Elizabeth Stadium with the popular Cantopop singer, Michael Kwan. She invited the Philharmonic to take part. I was initially reluctant but agreed, provided that she permitted the orchestra to play one work on its own. This was the main theme from John Williams's *Star Wars* suite. Following the success of these concerts, at the opening of the 12,000-seat Hong Kong Coliseum she again asked us to take part, this time with several singers including Michael Kwan, Liza Wang, and Danny Chan.

Buoyed by the success of these concerts, after discussion with my management team, we decided to present a programme of movie music in the Queen Elizabeth Stadium. This would include popular classical items from Hollywood films as well as some from Hong Kong films. I was thrilled when this sold out with almost 10,000 attending the three performances. Later in the year, we repeated the programme in the Coliseum with a greater variety of items and with the addition of a custom-designed specialist sound enhancement (amplification) system, and some simple lighting effects. We sold every one of the 35,000 seats available. I was delighted because I realised that some of those listening would eventually become more regular symphonic concert goers. From 1984 we presented four such Coliseum programmes each year with audience never dipping below 25,000. The most popular? Perhaps surprisingly, not one we presented with Leslie Cheung and Anita Mui, who were then just at the start of mega-stardom. It was a concert with the *Butterfly Lovers' Concerto*, the *Yellow River Concerto* and some popular themes from TV soap operas that we had orchestrated. We had to add two concerts for a total audience of nearly 52,000!

To reach a truly international audience, commercial recordings were essential. After discussions with Hong Kong–based Klaus Heymann, now best known worldwide for his Naxos label, we started with an experiment: an album of popular Chinese music titled *Colourful Clouds* excellently conducted by the young Hong Kong conductor then working in the United States, Kenneth Jean. So well did this sell that it was succeeded by *Under the Silver Moon* and an album of music by Hong Kong's most famous popular composer, Joseph Koo. Soon we branched into more classical repertoire with music by Richard Strauss, Glazunov, Villa-Lobos, and César Cui.

With Hong Kong's future after 1997 settled in late 1983, our Chairman Phillip Kwok suggested we consider a tour in the Chinese mainland. Accordingly, our assistant general manager (development and marketing) Tseng Sun-man and I set off for discussions with the China Performing Arts Agency (CPAA) in Beijing. This eventually resulted in a six-concert tour to Shanghai, Hangzhou and Beijing in February 1986. Although there were several disasters due to less-than-ideal planning by CPAA, the tour itself was a major success with praise all round from the Chinese and Hong Kong media.

By the time I left the Philharmonic in July 1986, we had indeed been able to increase the number of musicians to 84. Kenneth had been delighted to add Wagner to the orchestra's repertoire when he conducted *The Flying Dutchman* for the 1987 Hong Kong Arts Festival. As I have watched the progress of the Philharmonic over the years, I have been excited to hear of its continuing development. But never in my wildest dreams would I ever have thought it could perform and record Wagner's mighty *Ring* cycle. That it did so so triumphantly reflects enormous credit to those who have steered its development, particularly over the last two decades.

That I was given the opportunity of playing a very small part much earlier in its development fills me with much gratitude. I wish all involved on stage and backstage, including the HKSAR Government, the Swire Group and the others who give so generously, only the best of good fortune over the next fifty years.

John Duffus
General Manager (1979–1986)
Hong Kong Philharmonic Society Limited
September 2023

Photo 52.1: John Duffus at the Great Wall.

A Concert of Life

In 1974, the HK Phil became a professional orchestra. The plan for professionalisation was initiated during the inaugural Hong Kong Arts Festival in 1973. At the time, the Hong Kong Governor Sir Murray MacLehose described the process as one in which the orchestra was conceived and established in under a year, bringing dozens of concerts annually to Hong Kong – something that 'Hong Kong can be proud of.'

In 1974, I too began my professional journey, starting a position in the accounting department of a large company after graduation. By chance, I saw a recruitment advertisement for the 'Hong Kong Philharmonic Society'. At the time, I didn't even know what 'Philharmonic' meant. A quick dictionary lookup revealed it to mean 'deep love of music'. What it didn't explain, however, was that the Philharmonic Society was the organisation managing the orchestra. Having loved music since childhood – singing in school choirs and using part-time tutoring income to pay for piano lessons – I was eager to apply for a music-related job. The position also offered a generous four-figure monthly salary, which was highly attractive to someone just entering the workforce.

The recruitment process was no simple matter. It began with a written test held in a room at City Hall, attended by at least forty people. I was fortunate enough to make it to the interview stage. Facing me were Darwin Chen, the manager of City Hall, and a tall, commanding expatriate who I later learned was the renowned Maestro Hans Günter Mommer (HK Phil's principal conductor and musical director from 1975). I sensed they were looking for someone who loved music, and I was lucky to be selected to join the orchestra.

On my first day of work in 1975, I followed the address on my offer letter to the 'Second Floor, Low Block, City Hall'. However, even before stepping into the office, I encountered my first challenge! The second floor housed the balcony seating of the concert hall, adjacent to a Chinese restaurant. Where exactly was my office? It turned out that the newly established HK Phil had repurposed a dressing room in the concert hall as its office. To reach it, you had to pass through an unassuming door leading to a long corridor that also connected to the restaurant kitchen. The office was at the end of the corridor. At the time, the organisation consisted of only five staff members: General Manager So Hau-leung, Secretary Ho Siu-chi, Concert Assistant James Kwok, Office Assistant Ambrose Law, and me.

Before my arrival, accounting tasks were handled by Peter Chan Po Fun & Co. My first assignment was to take over their responsibilities. I'm deeply grateful to accountant Peter Chan for patiently teaching me and helping me establish the orchestra's first set of accounting ledgers. But my duties extended beyond numbers; they also involved numbers of words. In the 1970s, telegrams were still widely used and their cost-per-word structure demanded creative brevity. I frequently drafted telegrams for urgent communication with artists overseas, sending or decoding them at the Cable & Wireless Office, conveniently located opposite City Hall.

While the concert assistant primarily managed scores and assisted backstage during rehearsals and performances, the rest of us handled everything else: booking venues, scheduling artists, arranging flights and hotels, greeting artists at the airport, organising ticketing, handling banking matters and personnel issues in the orchestra. Despite the hectic workload, I thoroughly enjoyed the close-knit working environment. The location of our office within City Hall made it easy for musicians to drop by during rehearsal breaks. I saw every orchestra member at least once a month because back then, pay cheques were handed out in person, leading to more face-to-face interactions and a familial atmosphere.

As the orchestra grew, we moved from City Hall to a proper office in Causeway Bay. By 1982, our team had expanded to nine people under General Manager John Duffus. That year marked a turning point, as vice chairman of Urban Council, Hugh Moss Gerald Forsgate, approved a proposal to align HK Phil salaries with the government's master pay scale. This also led to an administrative restructuring. I was promoted to accounting and administration manager, alongside two other managers – orchestra personnel manager Lee Bo Luen and marketing and promotions manager Ethel Lau – marking the beginning of a departmental system. By 1983, I was further promoted to assistant general manager, along with Lee Bo Luen. Tseng Sun-man joined as development and marketing manager and was quickly promoted as well.

Under John Duffus's leadership, the orchestra flourished, achieving many milestones: reintroducing subscription ticket plans, establishing the Friends of the Philharmonic membership club to strengthen audience relationships, conducting its first China tour, forming the HK Phil Chorus, and creating the resident conductor position to facilitate regular school concerts. The entire administrative team functioned like sponges, constantly absorbing new knowledge and skills. Many who worked at HK Phil went on to shine in Hong Kong's cultural sector.

In 1989, HK Phil moved into the Cultural Centre – a momentous occasion. The author of this book, Jimmy Shiu, joined as audience development manager in late 1988, and we witnessed this pivotal moment together. I have particularly vivid memories of this year because I was pregnant at the time, yet I frequently had to rush around managing the progress of the office renovations. Despite the challenges, the joy of reuniting with the musicians in one location made it worthwhile. The new office was next to the concert hall, making operations much smoother. David Atherton, who had just become music director, even had his own office to facilitate artistic decision-making. An innovator, he also introduced Apple computers to our office, helping us set up in the new office. We gave him the nickname 'David Appleton'.

By 1994, as HK Phil celebrated its twentieth anniversary, I decided it was time to focus on family after nearly two decades of service. I thought this marked the end of my journey with the orchestra. However, it turned out to be just an intermission. After a short break and then working at the Consumer Council for twelve years, I returned to HK Phil in 2010, driven by my deep love for music and the orchestra.

It is impossible to compare the HK Phil today with the small family that grew from the dressing rooms of City Hall back in the day! Although my job title remains similar, the nature of the work has changed significantly. The departmental structure established years ago has now matured. Each department has a dedicated and hardworking team. The promotions and fundraising functions have split into two robust teams: the Development Department and the Marketing Department. HK Phil, now elevated to world-class artistic standards, offers a diverse repertoire and invites internationally acclaimed artists, necessitating an independent Artistic Planning Department to handle complex matters such as visas, contracts, itineraries, and programming – tasks that require professionals with expertise in music. What brings me the most joy is the opportunity to work once again with Stage Manager Steven Chan, who has served the orchestra since 1977. The Orchestral Operations team has grown into a critical nine-member department that manages the daily affairs of nearly a hundred orchestra members.

Unknowingly, I have worked at HK Phil for thirteen years now, facing challenges no less demanding than those in the past. The pandemic caused a global halt to the performing arts for several years but also pushed HK Phil to embrace the new digital era. In 2020, the orchestra performed the online edition of the Swire Symphony Under the Stars in the Cultural Centre Concert Hall without an audience under the baton of Resident Conductor Lio Kuokman, garnering remote support from audience worldwide. The most significant challenge was the ambitious *Ring* cycle concerts and recording project proposed by former chief executive Michael MacLeod. I vividly recall him coming to me with a serious expression to discuss 'something big': a plan to have the orchestra perform Wagner's *Ring* cycle over four years, with an immense budget requiring additional funding. Despite the odds, we overcame all challenges to accomplish a goal that few orchestras in the world can achieve. This project earned us not only recognition from Hong Kong audiences but also the prestigious Orchestra of the Year award from *Gramophone* magazine in 2019. The recordings are now available for free enjoyment in the Watch & Listen section of our website.

HK Phil's achievements today owe much to the efforts and support of many. The HKSAR government has consistently supported the orchestra through various mechanisms, allowing the public to enjoy world-class performances at relatively affordable prices. Additionally, the Swire Group, as the principal patron since 2006, has not only provided financial stability but also valuable guidance for the orchestra's development. Our shared commitment to community engagement has made the annual Swire Symphony Under the Stars a highly anticipated event for the people of Hong Kong. I must also express my gratitude to former Board Chairman Mr Y. S. Liu for his unwavering support. A violinist with the orchestra during its amateur days, Mr Liu has always been deeply devoted to HK Phil. Under his leadership, the orchestra achieved many milestones, such as European tours and the *Ring* cycle project mentioned earlier.

This year marks the HK Phil's fiftieth professional season. Reflecting on my journey – from a young newcomer to now approaching retirement – it feels like a lifetime has passed, yet it all seems to have gone by in the blink of an eye. Spanning the first half of my career with the orchestra (1975–1994) and the second half (2010–present), I am deeply grateful to have performed this thirty-three-year-long concert of life with the HK Phil.

It has been an extraordinary privilege to witness the continuous growth of an orchestra that truly belongs to Hong Kong over the past fifty years. I am immensely proud of how the HK Phil has evolved from its early days of professionalisation to becoming a world-class ensemble. Looking ahead, I hope the orchestra will have its own dedicated performance and rehearsal venue, continue to reach even greater artistic heights, and carry forward the legacy of being an orchestra 'Hong Kong can be proud of', inspiring pride among all its citizens.

Wishing you all good health and happiness!

Vennie Ho
Executive Director
Hong Kong Philharmonic Society Limited
December 2023[1]

Photo 52.2, Photo 52.3, and Photo 52.4: Vennie Ho with chief executives: John Duffus (top left), Benedikt Fohr (bottom left), and Michael MacLeod (right).

[1] After retiring, Vennie Ho continued to serve as the fiftieth anniversary consultant for the 2023/24 season from January 2024. In recognition of her dedication to the arts and culture of Hong Kong, she was awarded the Lifetime Achievement Award by the League of China Orchestras and Chief Executive's Commendation for Community Service in 2024.

Chairman and President

Chairman, Hong Kong Philharmonic Society (1974–1977)	The Hon. Alex S. C. Wu, CBE, LLD, JP
President (1974–1976) Honorary President (1976–2000) Hong Kong Philharmonic Society	The Hon. Sir Kenneth Ping-Fan Fung, CBE, LLD, DDOCSC, JP, KSTJ
Chairman, General Committee (1977–1981)	Mr John MacKenzie, JP
Chairman, Board of Governors (1978–2005)	Dr the Hon. Arnaldo de Oliveira Sales, GBM, OBE, CBE, JP, GCIH
Chairman, General Committee (1981–1991)	Dr Philip Kwok, SBS, JP
Honorary Vice President (1983–1992)	Dr. S. M. Bard, OBE, ED, JP
Chairman, General Committee (1991–1995)	The Hon. Marvin Cheung, GBS, OBE, JP
Chairman, General Committee (1995–1997)	Ms Ada Wong Ying-kay, JP
Chairman, General Committee (1997–2000)	Dr Patrick C. P. Ho, MD, FACS, GBS, JP
Acting Chairman, General Committee (2000–2002)	Dr Philip Kwok, SBS, JP
Chairman, General Committee (2002–2004)	Mr Hu Fa-kuang, GBM, GBS, CBE, JP

Chairman, General Committee (2004–2005)	Dr Geoffrey Yeh Meou-tsen, SBS, MBE, JP
Chairman, General Committee (2005–2006)	Mr Edward Ho Sing-tin, SBS, OBE, JP
Chairman, Board of Governors (2006)	The Hon. Marvin Cheung, GBS, OBE, JP
Chairman, Board of Governors (2006–2008)	Mr Edward Ho Sing-tin, SBS, OBE, JP
Chairman, Board of Governors (2008–2014)	Mr Y. S. Liu, MH
Chairman, Board of Governors (2014–2015)	The Hon. Jack So Chak Kwong, GBM, GBS, OBE, JP
Chairman, Board of Governors (2015–2021)	Mr Y. S. Liu, MH
Chairman, Board of Governors (2021–)	Mr David Cogman

Director and Conductor

Music Director and Principal Conductor (1974–1975)	Lim Kek-tjiang
Principal Conductor and Musical Director (1977–1978) Principal Conductor (1979)	Hans Günter Mommer
Music Director (1979–1982) Principal Guest Conductor (1982)	Ling Tung
Assistant Conductor (1980–1982)	Carl Pini
Principal Guest Conductor (1982–1985)	Maxim Shostakovich
Assistant Conductor (1983–1989)	Miran Kojian
Music Director (1984–1989)	Kenneth Schermerhorn
Principal Guest Conductor (1984–1993)	Kenneth Jean
Resident Conductor and Chorusmaster (1984–1986)	John Szicheng Lau
Principal Guest Conductor (1986)	Jorge Mester
Resident Conductor and Chorusmistress (1986–2000)	Yip Wing-sie, JP
Music Director (1989–2000) Conductor Laureate (2000–2009)	David Atherton, OBE

Music Director (2000–2003) Principal Conductor (2003–2005)	Samuel Wong
Resident Conductor (2001–2003)	Choi Ho-man
Artistic Director and Chief Conductor (2004–2012)	Edo de Waart
Resident Conductor (2005)	Harmen Cnossen
Assistant Conductor (2008–2010) Associate Conductor (2010–2012)	Perry So
Music Director (2012–2024)	Jaap van Zweden, SBS
Principal Guest Conductor (2015–)	Long Yu
Assistant Conductor (2016–2018)	Vivian Ip
Assistant Conductor (2016–2018)	Gerard Salonga
Resident Conductor (2020–)	Lio Kuokman, JP
Artistic Partner (2024–2025)	Daniele Gatti
Music Director (2026–)	Tarmo Peltokoski

Concertmaster and Leader

Leader (1974–1976) Acting Concertmaster (1977)	Lim Kek-tin
Leader (1977) Concertmaster (1977–1980)	Jan van den Berg
Concertmaster (1979)	Ben Hudson
Concertmaster (1980)	Vincent Frittelli
Concertmaster (1980–1982)	Carl Pini
Concertmaster (1982–1989)	Miran Kojian
Concertmaster (1989–1990)	Jae Park
Acting Concertmaster (1991)	Fan Ting
Guest Concertmasters (1992)	Jan van den Berg John Georgiadis Leo Philips
Concertmaster (1992–1993)	Michael Ma
Concertmaster (1993–2000)	Barry Wilde
Concertmaster (2000–2005)	Dennis Kim Jin-soo
Concertmaster (2006–2011)	John Harding
Concertmaster (2012–2013)	Igor Yuzefovich
Concertmaster (2013–)	Jing Wang

Hong Kong Philharmonic Orchestra (Season 2025/26)

Music Director Designate	Tarmo Peltokoski
Principal Guest Conductor	Long Yu
Resident Conductor	Lio Kuokman
Composer-in-Residence	Esa-Pekka Salonen
Concertmaster	Jing Wang
First Associate Concertmaster	Leung Kin-fung
Second Associate Concertmaster	Anders Hui
Second Associate Concertmaster	Wang Liang
Third Associate Concertmaster	Bei de Gaulle

First Violins
Ai Jin
Ba Wenjing
Cheng Li
Gui Li
Jia Shuchen
Li Zhisheng
Liu Fangxi
Mao Hua
Rachael Mellado
Zhang Xi

Second Violins

Zhao Yingna●
Domas Juškys■
Leslie Moonsun Ryang▲
Fang Jie
Gallant Ho Ka-leung
Liu Boxuan
Mao Yiguo
Katrina Rafferty
Miyaka Suzuki Wilson
Tomoko Tanaka
Christine Wong
Zhang Yuchen
Zhou Tengfei

Violas

Andrew Ling●
Li Jiali■
Kaori Wilson▲
Cui Hongwei
Fu Shuimiao
Ethan Heath
Li Ming
Damara Lomdaridze
Alice Rosen
Sun Bin
Zhang Shuying

Cellos

Richard Bamping●
Fang Xiaomu■
Dora Lam▲
Chan Ngat-chau
Chen Yi-chun
Timothy Frank
Anna Kwan Ton-an
Haedeun Lee
Tae-mi Song
Song Yalin

Double Basses

George Lomdaridze●
Jiang Xinlai◆
Chang Pei-heng
Feng Rong
Samuel Ferrer
Jeffrey Lehmberg
Philip Powell
Jonathan Van Dyke

Flutes

Megan Sterling●
Olivier Nowak■
Josep Portella Orfila

Piccolo

Linda Stuckey◆

Oboes
Michael Wilson●
Wang Yu-po■
Marrie Rose Kim

Cor Anglais
Kwan Sheung-fung◆

Clarinets
Andrew Simon●
John Schertle■
Lau Wai

Bass Clarinet
Lorenzo Iosco◆

Bassoons
Benjamin Moermond●
Toby Chan■
Vance Lee◆

Contrabassoon
Adam Treverton Jones◆

Horns
Lin Jiang●
Russell Bonifede■
Chow Chi-chung▲
Todor Popstoyanov
Homer Lee
Jorge Medina

Trumpets
Nitiphum Bamrungbanthum●
Christopher Moyse■
Douglas Waterston
Robert Smith

Trombones
Jarod Vermette●
Christian Goldsmith
Kevin Thompson

Bass Trombone
Aaron Albert◆

Tuba
Paul Luxenberg●

Timpani
James Boznos●

Percussion
Aziz D. Barnard Luce●
Raymond Leung Wai-wa
Sophia Woo Shuk-fai

Harp
Woojin Lee●

● Principal
■ Co-Principal
◆ Associate Principal
▲ Assistant Principal

Hong Kong Philharmonic Society Limited

Bernhard Fleischer	Chief Executive
Patrick Ren	Deputy Chief Executive
Sophia Sun	Executive Assistant

Administration and Finance

Homer Lee	Director of Administration & Finance
Iris Kwok	Finance Manager
Andrew Li	IT & Project Manager
Annie Ng	Human Resources Manager
Alex Kwok	Assistant Administration & Finance Manager
Vinchi Cheung	IT Project Coordinator
Crystal Fung	Senior Human Resources Officer
Rachel Go	Administrative Officer
Monarch Kwok*	Arts Administration Trainee

Artistic Planning

Timothy Tsukamoto	Director of Artistic Planning

Charlotte Chiu	Education & Outreach Manager
Michelle Wong	Artistic Planning Manager
Ashley Chin*	Assistant Project Manager
Gloria Tang	Assistant Artistic Planning Manager
Kent Lam	Education & Outreach Officer
Hilary Wong*	Education & Outreach Officer
Ellie To*	Programme Officer
Jennifer Wong*	Project Officer

Development

Debora Cheng	Director of Development
Vanessa Leung	Development Manager
Jennifer Tung	Development Manager
Simon Hung	Assistant Development Manager
Jen Lam	Assistant Development Manager
Hester Cheng	Development Officer

Marketing

Dennis Wu	Director of Marketing
Emily Hui	Media Relations & Communications Manager
Emily Leung	Digital Marketing & CRM Manager
Michelle Yeung	Marketing Manager
Joshua Tsui	Publications Editor
Olivia Chau	Assistant Marketing Manager
Michelle Lee	Assistant Ticketing Manager
Joanne Chan*	Archivist
Jessica Ho	Marketing Officer – Customer Service & Ticketing
Jane Wong	Marketing Officer

Orchestral Operations

Vanessa Chan	Director of Orchestral Operations
Betty Ho	Librarian
Camille Tam	Stage & Production Manager
Joseph Wong	Orchestra Personnel Manager

Chan Tim-yan	Assistant Librarian
Apple Li	Assistant Orchestral Operations Manager
Cobby Siu	Assistant Orchestral Operations Manager
Arthur Lo	Producer (Digital Media & Special Projects)
Lee Lok-yin	Senior Stage & Production Officer
Tiffany Chan*	Stage & Production Intern

*Contract Staff

Acknowledgements

Names are listed in alphabetical order by surname.

Esther Chan
Joanne Chan
Ka Wai Chan
Mimi Chan
Steven Chan
Toby Chan
Vanessa Chan
Chan Wing Wah
Jim Chang
Darwin Chen
Meggy Cheng
Rachel Cheung
Samson Cheung
Charlotte Chiu
Raymond Choi
Oliver Chou
Leon Chu
Aurora Corpus
Ernesto Corpus
John Duffus
Fan Ting
Benedikt Fohr
Allistar Gaskin
David Gwilt
Betty Ho
Harris Ho
Vennie Ho
Mark Hui
Haider Kikabhoy
Joe Kirtley
Kwan Kin-sang
Nelson Lai
Kathy Lam
Kuno Lam
Grace Lang
Ethel Lau
Savio Lau
Ambrose Law
Daniel Law
Lee Bo-luen
Colleen Lee
Homer Lee

Lee Wai-fook
Warren Lee
Leung Bo-kun
Leung Kin-fung
Raymond Leung
Vanessa Leung
Leung Wai-kit
Eric Li
Lio Kuokman
Jacqueline Liu
Y. S. Liu
Carrie Lo
Lo King-man
Rocky Lok
Nancy Loo
Roger Manners
Christopher Moyse
Jaren Ng
Leanne Nicholls
Martin Poon
Solomon Shiu
Andrew Simon
So Hau-leung
Paul Tam
Tin Wing-sin
Tseng Sun-man
Jonathan Van Dyke
Jing Wang
Wang Liang
Walter Wong
Sophia Woo
Dennis Wu
Yip Wing-sie

Composers and Authors Society of Hong Kong

Hong Kong Central Library

As well as other Hong Kong Philharmonic Orchestra players and staff who contributed to the production of this book.

HK Phil 50+

A Hong Kong Philharmonic Orchestra Project

Author: Jimmy Shiu

Consultant: Vennie Ho

Cover design adapted from the Chinese edition, originally designed by Kaman Cheng

Photos: Unless otherwise specified, photos are provided by HK Phil, HK Phil Archive, and photographers Desmond Chan, Olivia Chau, Cheung Chi Wai, Cheung Wai Lok, Keith Hiro, Eric Hong, Issac Wong, and Ka Lam.

Published by:
Hong Kong University Press
The University of Hong Kong
Pok Fu Lam Road
Hong Kong

https://hkupress.hku.hk

Digitally printed

First Edition. December 2025.

Price: HK$198

ISBN: 978-988-8900-94-7

© 2025 Hong Kong Philharmonic Society Limited. All rights reserved.
Unauthorised reproduction is prohibited.

The Hong Kong Philharmonic Orchestra is financially supported by the Government of the Hong Kong Special Administrative Region.

Principal Patron: Swire